A WORLD OF
IMPACT

CARA FRANCE AND THE CEOS
OF YPO GOLDEN GATE

A WORLD OF IMPACT

STORIES FROM CEOS ON
HOW YPO HELPS THEM **THRIVE**

LIONCREST
PUBLISHING

A WORLD OF IMPACT
Stories from CEOs on How YPO Helps Them Thrive

ISBN   978-1-5445-3499-2 *Hardcover*
       978-1-5445-0379-0 *Paperback*
       978-1-5445-0378-3 *Ebook*

To the CEOs of YPO Golden Gate who
courageously challenge the status quo.

Contents

PART THREE: BUILDING RELATIONSHIPS

PART FOUR: DIVERSE PERSPECTIVES

The Complex Life of a CEO

THERE'S NO DOUBT ABOUT IT: LEADING A COMPANY today is an honor and a privilege, especially in these dynamic and exciting times. Today's CEO has a unique opportunity to impact lives, industries, and the world in very real ways. It is a position many aspire to but few achieve. It is both all-consuming and deeply rewarding.

That doesn't mean the life of a CEO is easy. In fact, it tends to be both difficult and complex. Not only is it demanding to successfully lead and grow a business, but it is also often challenging to balance professional responsibilities with other aspects of life, such as family, relationships, and personal growth.

Many CEOs find themselves feeling isolated, with few to turn to during those times when they could benefit from guidance, input, or even an empathetic ear. It is for this reason that the Young Presidents' Organization (YPO) was founded about seventy years ago. In 1950, Ray Hickok found himself heading up his family's 300-employee company. He was just twenty-seven at the time. Presumably, there weren't many people he could talk to about his experiences, because there weren't many people *in* his position in the first place—particularly within his peer group.

For the sake of solidarity, insight, and support, Hickok set up what would be the first of thousands of YPO meetings. Eventually, these meetings would span the globe. But this first one happened at the Waldorf Astoria in New York City and consisted of a small group of men, including General Robert Johnson, the head of Johnson & Johnson at the time. The first meeting was a success, so the group began meeting regularly to share ideas, insights, and experiences—peer to peer.

Times have changed, but the experience of leadership has not. The challenges and pressures CEOs face today are no different from when Hickok initiated that first meeting in 1950. While business complexity has exploded, the personal experience of a CEO—and the emotional challenges of the role—remain unchanged.

Today, YPO is the largest network of business leaders in the world. It has spread across 130 countries and grown to include more than 26,000 innovative leaders. Its membership consists of individuals who have become the president, chairman, or CEO of a significant organization before the age of forty-five, and many are much younger. This age limit means not only are YPO members running significant businesses at a relatively young age, but they are also in the thick of life, balancing professional duties with relationships, family, and personal growth.

At the heart of YPO is the notion of the "whole self." Leaders gather in YPO to share business insights and lessons while also helping each other find balance, navigate life, and continue to grow as people, community members, parents, partners, and spouses.

You Don't Have to Be Alone

It might sound like a cliché, but it can be lonely at the top, especially when you reach the top early in life. No matter how many people you have in your life, few can truly understand the demands and complexities of your situation. Not your spouse or friends. Not your coworkers. Not your board of directors. Your spouse and friends have your best interests at heart, but chances are, they've never run a multimillion-dollar company. Your coworkers don't necessarily see issues from the same vantage point. And your board is primarily focused on shareholder value. It's tempting to feel that you are, in many ways, alone.

YPO dissolves that sense of isolation by bringing together peers to talk, learn, share, and support each other's personal growth. Most importantly, it offers a safe space within which to do so. Confidentiality is the foundation of YPO because it enables members to share experiences—whether personal or professional—in a real, unvarnished, deep way. Nothing is off limits.

YPO provides its members access to the accumulated wisdom, life experiences, and lessons of the extended community. It offers a confidential environment for the type of mentorship, fellowship, and guidance that is otherwise difficult to glean from people in similar situations. This counsel can illuminate opportunities and flag blind spots before you realize they exist. With this practical and insightful advice, good leaders can grow into great leaders and, in the process, become an example for others to follow.

As a leader, you impact a lot of people—not only your employ-ees and customers but also your investors, vendors, partners, suppliers, and colleagues. *And this is just in your work life.* CEOs also have myriad commitments outside of work, which doesn't leave much time for personal reflection and growth.

YPO provides time for that growth—and so much more. YPO provides members with the rare opportunity to continually evolve on a holistic level. It makes you *better* on all levels. When *you* evolve, everyone *around you* is positively affected.

YPO is about more than leadership. It's about life. Leaders are merely people trying to navigate life in the best way possible, like anyone else, and YPO offers them a unique opportunity to share, connect, and grow.

How It Works

YPO is an international organization, with 450 chapters around the globe. Chapters range from 30 to more than 200 members. Each chapter consists of several forums, with eight to twelve members per forum. These forums meet nine or ten times per year, and each meeting is about four hours long. These "forum meetings" are self-moderated, with a specific, structured way of sharing and exploring issues that lead to connection and growth for the individual and the forum as a whole. Each fo-rum has an annual retreat that is often run by a highly skilled facilitator.

Forums are the heart of YPO because your forum mates are gen-erally the people you know best and with whom you share the most. YPO members typically cite forum as the most critical and important aspect of their YPO experience. Some forums rotate members over time, while others keep the same members for decades. While forum structure varies, YPO strives to have forums remain together for long enough that members have an opportunity to achieve real depth and growth.

In addition to forums, each chapter creates one-of-a-kind social and educational events, with themes such as education, personal growth, peak experiences, business insights, and executive learning. These events are often referred to as "Only in YPO" because they present a unique opportunity for YPO members to learn from otherwise inaccessible content experts and industry leaders. For example, the Golden Gate chapter recently had the opportunity to meet with several members of the US Supreme Court at the height of the historic Brett Kavanaugh hearings. Another trip involved an adventure to New Orleans, where YPO members learned how to prepare for a crisis of great magnitude from key business and civic leaders in the aftermath of Hurricane Katrina.

And there's more: YPO offers opportunities for partners and children to participate. It offers partner forums for spouses of YPO members and includes partners in most of the chapter educational and social events. Children have access to opportunities to visit some of today's leading companies through events such as Youth Learning About Business (YLAB), in addition to travel opportunities and various family-based events. Given that a CEO's life is so busy and demanding, YPO views carving out this family time as a critical aspect of its whole-self philosophy.

Because of YPO's international footprint, members can look up a local YPO chapter anywhere on the planet and easily meet with people leading local businesses, communities, cities, and even countries. Since the confidentiality clause and forum experience are consistent around the globe, an immediate level of depth in conversation is the norm. The opportunity to have authentic, earnest conversations about real and sometimes sensitive topics in the course of otherwise random encounters is an incredible benefit of YPO.

Innovation in the Bay

This book highlights insights and experiences from members of YPO's Golden Gate chapter, which is located in the San Francisco Bay Area—from Silicon Valley to Napa Valley and from the East Bay to the Golden Gate Bridge. Over time, the Golden Gate chapter has earned a reputation for being one of the most diverse and forward-thinking chapters in YPO.

In many ways, this is not surprising. Since the days of the 1849 Gold Rush, there has been a history in this part of California of trying and failing, then trying again—always going for it and constantly trying something new. It was here the Human Potential Movement sprang to life, and here some of today's most innovative and disruptive companies have laid down their roots. Game-changing tech leaders such as Apple, Facebook, Uber, Airbnb, Twitter, Netflix, and Google call the Bay Area home. In many ways, the YPO Golden Gate chapter is an extension of the experimental Bay Area zeitgeist.

Diversity is also one of the defining characteristics of YPO Golden Gate—diversity of culture, gender, business, and perspective. These divergent backgrounds, sensibilities, and experiences coalesce to support each member in being better informed, more enriched, and capable of appreciating a broad spectrum of perspectives. This pays dividends in any number of ways, both professional and personal.

In 1950, diversity was not necessarily a word associated with YPO, mostly because back then, there was not much diversity in YPO or leadership. As the world evolved and leaders with diverse backgrounds stepped forward, the face of YPO shifted. This shift is occurring in various ways and at various speeds, depending on the culture of the region where a given YPO chapter is located and the leadership of each chapter.

Until recently, most YPO forums were not co-ed. There were simply not enough women in the organization to intersperse within forums. Some believed a same-sex environment allowed members to speak more easily, freely, and authentically. This perspective is rapidly changing, and YPO's Golden Gate chapter is leading the way as the first chapter globally to have 100 percent of its member and partner forums be mixed-gender. This shift to co-ed forums has produced amazing results. Members gain insight, perspective, and awareness on completely new topics and, in the end, find themselves going *deeper* than in same-sex forums. Exchanges are more nuanced and richer, encompassing a wider range of viewpoints. Thanks to the chapter's holistic co-ed approach, YPO Golden Gate members report they experience real, sustainable growth—both as leaders and as *people*—whether that means being a better spouse, a better parent, or a better citizen. There's no doubt about it: diversity is a competitive advantage.

Finding Time to Grow

Time is the biggest challenge for most people considering YPO membership. Finding balance in life is difficult, even more so as a CEO. Already, there are not enough hours in the day, and it can be overwhelming to contemplate allocating an additional half a day every month to yet another obligation.

What YPO members have found to be true, however, again and again, is that carving out time for YPO creates tremendous benefits in the long run. As you will see throughout these pages, the YPO experience provides the sort of insight, information, and personal support that gives leaders the power to shift and reprioritize. Members are actually able to accomplish more on every level and feel better and more centered in the process.

It's one thing to tell you this. It's better to see what it looks like in practice. Throughout this book, dozens of CEOs just like you share stories about how the YPO experience transformed their lives. Not only has it served as a catalyst for growth and evolution for them, but it has also served as a game-changer in tangible, deeply meaningful ways. The stories are grouped into four categories: Lessons in Leadership, Nurturing Your Whole Self, Building Relationships, and Diverse Perspectives.

YPO will support your growth to be a great CEO, and it will provide so much more.

CARA FRANCE
Co-founder and CEO, The Sage Group
Member of YPO Golden Gate

CHAPTER ONE

Why YPO Matters

Cara France, Co-founder and CEO of
The Sage Group and Creator of Marketers
That Matter®

Recognized as one of the San Francisco Bay Area's largest women-owned businesses, Cara has grown The Sage Group into an award-winning professional services firm that provides marketing consultants, contractors, and permanent talent to leading companies. Clients include dozens of Silicon Valley's premier technology companies, largest banks, and top global brands.

Inc. magazine has recognized Sage as one of the fastest-growing companies in America twice in the past decade. Cara was recognized as Woman Entrepreneur of the Year in 2011 by the Women's Initiative, receiving special congressional recognition from Rep. Nancy Pelosi, and was an Ernst & Young Winning Women Finalist in 2012. Cara is a regular contributor to the Harvard Business Review, authoring numerous articles focused on leadership, strategy, and marketing insights.

FOR AS LONG AS I CAN REMEMBER, I'VE WANTED TO BE an entrepreneur; however, it still took a while for me to find my path.

Right out of college, I worked as a management consultant at a top East Coast firm. I worked long hours, usually seven days a week. Although I'm a people person, I had little time to do anything but sleep after work. I was completely out of alignment.

After leaving that job in DC, I moved to California to attend business school at Stanford, where I could learn more about entrepreneurship and discover more about who I was as a leader. Although I took classes from well-respected professors, there was minimal discussion of entrepreneurial models outside raising venture capital or private equity funding for a scalable global business, commonly referred to as the "zero-billion-dollar business." Small startup-services businesses were not on the menu.

A few years after business school, the internet was taking off, and I joined a "hot" startup. Six months in, the company's culture devolved into toxic turf wars. The culture and my participation in it felt antithetical to who I wanted to be. So, with $80,000 in business school debt, no backup opportunity, and the belief that I was walking away from millions, I quit. I couldn't bear the thought of working there another day. When I finally left, I wasn't even sure who my boss was. A week and a half later, the company ran out of money, and everyone was laid off *without* receiving their final paychecks (yes, that is illegal).

Even though I was still in my twenties, I felt I'd already spent too much time in places that didn't "fit" me. What I didn't see clearly until later was that each of these environments was, for me, a fundamental mismatch. My management consultant role required me to crunch numbers in huge spreadsheets (I once ran Excel out of memory) when what I really thrived on was working with people and thinking creatively. And the "hot" startup was really a "hot mess," brimming with hubris, infighting, grandstanding, and backstabbing—not my cup of tea either. However, there was a plus side to these misadventures: they helped me hone my core values and begin understanding what mattered most to me.

Building (and Rebuilding) Businesses

I finally decided it was time to chase down my entrepreneurial desires. My first company was an online store for handcrafted artisan gifts—a bit like the Etsy of its time. The process of creating that company was energizing, but soon, reality set in. Online stores are all about shipping and merchandising, and I quickly learned I hated both of those things. Plus, I spent many days working alone, which just wasn't me. Here, I learned another important lesson: I thrive when partnering with others.

Eventually, I found my way back to consulting and got into a rhythm that combined a blend of marketing and strategy. I worked four days a week, got paid relatively well, and could see a new trend on the horizon. Even though this was long before people started talking about the "gig economy," I surmised that careers would become less linear and business would continue to become more project-based.

This gave me an idea. I got together with a business school colleague, and we started a company to provide marketing and business consultants to San Francisco Bay Area companies. Thus, The Sage Group was born.

From the beginning, my partner and I worked hard on values, goals, alignment, and communication because we knew those were the foundational elements of our new company that would get us through the tough times. For about a year, they did. Our business achieved some traction, but I could sense something was off with my partner. He finally admitted his heart wasn't in the business and he wanted to move on.

My first entrepreneurial venture had already taught me never to start a business by myself. Now I found myself with a growing business and no partner. When he told me he wanted to leave, I remember going into my closet, curling up into the fetal position, and bawling my eyes out. I then woke the next morning and kept moving forward.

One step at a time, I grew The Sage Group into what it is today.

Downward Spiral

By the fall of 2008, the company was five years old and thriving, with revenues of $10 million. We were finishing an RFP with our largest client. We knew everyone on the marketing side of the organization and had formed meaningful relationships up and down the company. What I didn't realize was the procurement guy was really running the show. I hadn't worked to make him an advocate, and it cost my company dearly.

One day, he called me to ask about pricing, and my attitude wasn't in check. I thought we were negotiating price, and my annoyance was palpable. My attitude gave him the excuse he was looking for. Weeks later, I got a phone call from one of our hiring managers. Their updated vendor list was distributed internally, and Sage wasn't on it. No matter how much I escalated and cajoled, the decision was final. To make matters worse, three weeks later in 2008, the Great Recession started, and our clients quickly let many Sage consultants go. Almost overnight, 80 percent of our business was gone.

I was forty years old, and most of our revenue was up in smoke, with no relief in sight. I felt like I couldn't breathe. For a few weeks, I felt like throwing in the towel, closing up shop, and moving to Bali. At home, however, I had a supportive husband, who has been through numerous startups himself, and our beautiful three-year-old twins. My wanderlust soon faded.

As we entered 2009, I went into the office each day forcing a smile. I got through that year by visualizing what it could look like on the other side of rebuilding, falling back on tremendous emotional support from family and friends.

That year, 2009, is the one year out of fifteen that Sage was not profitable—at least financially. Emotionally, personally, and professionally, it was extremely profitable. As difficult as that time was, I'm grateful for what I learned. If everything hadn't blown up, taking the company to the brink of disaster, I might not have stepped up to the plate to rebuild it into what it has become today.

And I might not have found YPO.

Getting to Know YPO

The next several years were about rebuilding the company from the ground up. By the beginning of 2011, we had fought our way back to $10 million in annual revenue. However, this time, we had a diversified client list, a robust sales team, a solid recruiting team, and a growing headcount.

During those same years, our industry faced strong headwinds. Placement was becoming commoditized, with intermediary, software-based personnel vetting causing tremendous downward pricing pressure. Several of Sage's competitors went out of business. I was the only executive at Sage, and I was physically, emotionally, spiritually, and mentally fried. It took a toll, and for the first time in my life, I started having full-blown panic attacks.

During this challenging time, I had tremendous support from my husband and family. And I was lucky enough to run across an amazing woman named Chris Yelton, a talented executive who joined Sage to help me grow the business. Finally, after so many years, I got a great business partner. Chris took on running the day-to-day operations, while I set out to find something that would differentiate Sage from its competitors. Until that point, we'd done the same thing as every company in our industry. Chris and I knew that wouldn't be enough for long.

It was right around this time I first heard about YPO through a random cold call from a Bay Area executive, Elizabeth Hutt Pollard, who was the membership officer for the YPO Golden Gate chapter. A few weeks later, she invited me to lunch. We hit it off instantly, and she put me on a fast track to membership.

Preconceived Notions

At the time, women comprised only 10 percent of the YPO Golden Gate chapter, and Elizabeth was committed to significantly increasing that percentage. For much of my career, I'd been a female executive in male-dominated companies, and I'd often felt I had to leave half of myself at the door. Joining a high-profile, male-dominated organization didn't seem like a smart move. If I was going to share deeply with people in the organization—and I intended to—I wanted to feel comfortable. I wanted *all* of me to be welcome.

Not only was I worried that 90 percent of the members were

men, but I was also concerned I might be walking into another "hot mess" of conceit, arrogance, and pretense. That is always a risk in organizations comprised of highly accomplished people in positions of power. Would I really find like-minded people in YPO?

Ultimately, my husband, Scott, helped me move past my concerns. Having been a CEO himself for many years, he understood something I couldn't yet see: the value of the YPO network. He knew how big the opportunity was, and his encouragement pushed me off the fence.

The presentation was daunting: ten minutes to present "all of myself" in front of a dozen accomplished CEOs. I presented my business—who we are, what we do, and who we serve. I also included slides of my abstract paintings, crazy yoga moves, intimate times with my family, and unusual friends from very different walks of life who have inspired me over the years.

At the end of the presentation, I answered their questions. Then they asked me if I had any questions for them. I did. "I don't think I'm a typical CEO," I said. "Will all of me be welcome here?"

In response, the CEO at the head of the table turned his notes around to show me the three words he'd scribbled as I gave my presentation. He'd written *artistic*, *spiritual*, and *creative*. He told me that those qualities were ones that he wanted to see more of in the Golden Gate chapter and that specifically *because* of who I was, I would be a valued part of the organization.

I was accepted into YPO, and within three weeks, I attended my first retreat. It was time to get to know the other CEOs—it was time to put this organization to the test.

I'll Have What She's Having

It had barely been a month since my first lunch with Elizabeth, which is warp speed for the YPO membership process, and there I was at my first members-only retreat. It felt strange at first, but everyone was welcoming.

"Would you like some wine?"

"No, thank you," I told them. "I only drink tequila."

I'm not a big drinker, but it's true—when I *do* drink, it's usually tequila. As you might imagine, it was a great way to break the ice. I quickly found that my fellow YPO members were not just welcoming but genuinely curious about who I was. They wanted to get to know me, and it showed in our conversations. We didn't engage in superficial small talk like you might expect at a cocktail party. Instead, conversations were brimming with powerful, authentic sharing.

What surprised me most was how comfortable I felt bringing my whole self to the table with both the women and the men of YPO. We were adding value to each other, and the philosophy held true that once you join, everyone is equal.

At that retreat, I also started getting to know my forum. I was immediately impressed with their talents and accomplishments—two ran publicly traded companies; more than half sat on public boards; another sat on President Obama's White House Council for Community Solutions; two were female; one was born and raised outside the United States; three had started their own company; one was a physician.

Even more impressive was who they were as people. They cared about the broader impact they were having on the world—being the best leaders, parents, and spouses they could be and attempting to add value in their communities. They brought humility and vulnerability that I'd rarely seen in business settings.

Real People, Real Benefits

I love the collaboration and support throughout the YPO organization. My friends from YPO reach out to me to ask for help personally and professionally, and I do the same. We trust each other and have each other's backs.

By 2013, two years after I joined YPO, I had figured out a way to truly differentiate Sage. We created and launched a program called Marketers That Matter® (MTM), a community of top marketing executives and companies. I leveraged many YPO connections in those early days to ask for introductions and support as we put together our first group of CMOs and sponsors.

After an initial meeting with an executive at the *Wall Street Journal* who expressed interest in being a sponsor, I lined up a phone call with a YPO mate who ran sponsorships at the Olympics, the World Cup, and other global sporting events. In less than thirty minutes, he gave me all the answers I needed about how to structure the deal.

MTM has grown into a premier membership organization with dozens of top brands and CMOs, millions in revenue, and ten *Harvard Business Review* articles inspired by the MTM community.

Building leadership skills and connections is not the only

benefit that I've gained from YPO. A CEO is a CEO every day, even when times get tough. You can't suddenly decide to take a break. This was especially evident when our daughter was admitted to the hospital when she was nine and a half. She had large kidney stones, which is extremely rare for kids. What started as one surgery turned into two months in and out of the hospital.

During that time, our daughter went through two major surgeries, three minor surgeries, three blood transfusions, and nine days on hospital bed rest with a catheter. Meanwhile, I was expected to be on stage for the MTM annual awards. I was simultaneously coauthoring an article for the *Harvard Business Review* and getting quotes from executives while my husband and I were running back and forth from the hospital.

I leaned hard on my YPO forum, especially on my forum mate who was a physician. When I learned our daughter would need a blood transfusion, I went into a panic. I associated blood transfusions with people who died. He reassured me that wasn't the case. Others in the group came to visit us in the hospital. Many of them let me cry on their shoulder.

I'm grateful for my friends at YPO—and that's what they are: *friends*. We share so much of ourselves on such a deep level that I think of my forum mates more as siblings. I care about their success and happiness, and I feel responsible for helping them find clarity when they're struggling. I want their lives to work on every level.

There are strict rules against dating within a YPO forum, and there are rules against conducting business within a forum. There are rules about confidentiality and conflicts of interest. YPO is a safe haven to explore and grow.

I believe men and women are different; we tend to look at
the world differently and lead differently. I also believe that
men and women are better off when they work together. Our
diversity is our strength. Every person in my YPO group is
unique, which adds depth to our perspectives. I love to hear
how different people experience the world in different ways.
The ability to hear these diverse perspectives enhances our
compassion and broadens our viewpoints.

PART ONE

LESSONS IN LEADERSHIP

CHAPTER TWO

Seeing around Corners

Kira Wampler, CEO of Art.com

Kira joined Art.com Inc. as its CEO in 2016. She previously worked in Silicon Valley for more than twenty years, primarily in marketing and product leadership. As the CMO at Lyft, Kira built the brand into a household name in a highly competitive and complex environment. Before Lyft, Kira was the CMO and head of the consumer business at Trulia, where she launched the company's first national marketing campaign and led all consumer product and marketing efforts. Before Trulia, she was the vice president of product and marketing at Lytro, where she led marketing, product, sales, and international growth and built a new category from the ground up.

I WAS AWARE OF YPO LONG BEFORE I BECAME A CEO. I first heard about it when I worked as an intern at Intuit, where Steven Aldrich, a senior executive, was a member of YPO. Years later, when I was the CMO at Trulia, the CEO, Pete Flint, was also a part of YPO. Pete and Steven were both members of the Golden Gate chapter, and I could tell YPO was valuable to them.

I didn't think about joining myself, though, until my last day as CMO of Lyft. I was attending an event hosted by Cara, and when I told her I'd just accepted the job as CEO of Art.com, her first reaction was "You have to join YPO!"

As I went through the interview and membership committee process for YPO, I realized that I already knew quite a few people in the group. It was reassuring to see a lot of familiar faces, so when I formally became a member and went to my first event, I wasn't intimidated in any way. Everyone was so warm and welcoming. It was easy for me to join the YPO family.

Support for CEOs

In my early years as an executive, when my goal was to eventually become a CEO myself, I often picked my bosses' brains about the types of mistakes new CEOs are prone to making. I wanted to know the common pitfalls so that I could avoid them when the time came.

What I learned time and again was that the best CEOs surround themselves with a private and confidential network of other CEOs. There is no substitute for the type of practical and actionable advice colleagues like that can provide. You can count on your spouse to support you, but they might not understand what it means to run a business. And while you can rely on board members for many things, there are a lot of topics on which it helps to have neutral feedback and support. For obvious reasons, you also can't merely go to some public conference and expect to get straight talk from another CEO about leading teams and managing transformation.

You need wise confidants. You need people who have been through what you're going through. You need to be able to have deep, revealing conversations.

So when I was approached to consider YPO, I jumped at the chance.

The Challenges at Art.com

My previous jobs had given me a wide range of experience. As CMO at Trulia, I had product, marketing, and engineering rolled up to me, and my job was to prioritize their time to drive the consumer side of the marketplace. At Lytro, I ran product, sales, marketing, and international; at Intuit, I learned how to become a mini-GM managing the QuickBooks Accountant Edition brand. At Lyft, I focused more on a narrow set of traditional marketing activities, given that was where all the challenges were in the early days of Lyft. From scaling up passengers and drivers to expanding to 300 cities, I focused heavily on growth and performance marketing while at the same time growing brand awareness and making the Lyft brand differentiated but accessible.

My time as a CMO made me feel ready for more end-to-end accountability. That's when CEO opportunities started to come my way, and I had the chance to move to Art.com.

I became CEO of Art.com in December 2016. The company has the world's most extensive assortment of art online as well as extraordinarily scaled operations and an excellent margin structure. However, over the years, the company had lost its way on customer experience and modern growth. I had some work to do.

To make matters more challenging, my first day on the job was Cyber Monday 2016. Online penetration for art is somewhere between 5 and 7 percent, compared to apparel, which is closer to 30 percent. It's difficult for customers to articulate a preference in art. When someone has art in their home, they will typically tell you they fell in love with the piece when they first saw it. That connection is tough to replicate online, so our challenge is to help people discover great art online and inspire them to buy it. Art is still in the early days of its e-commerce journey.

All of this is also why the job of leading the company was so appealing. Art.com is data rich, which is good news because we can use that data to make better decisions. What's more, customer experience and modern growth are my sweet spots, so this role was an opportunity for me to transform a business based on my areas of strength. I was also excited about the potential for developing the team at Art.com, both in terms of stretching the skills and approaches of the existing, longtime employees and bringing in fresh experiences from new leaders and team members.

New Demands

For as many questions as I'd asked earlier in my career and as much experience as I had, I quickly realized that I still had a great deal to learn about being a CEO.

As a CEO, a broad set of topics and issues consume your time. End-to-end accountability requires tremendous responsibility and a strong sense of prioritization. You're in charge of prioritizing not just your own time but everyone's time and ensuring the entire team is focused on the right priorities for the highest impact. This is particularly true of a company going through a transformation, where nearly everything needs to be modernized.

A CEO faces a different set of decisions than anyone else in the company. A CMO or GM makes choices just for their division, and they are surrounded by good people, including a CEO who can guide and support them through difficult decisions.

CEOs, on the other hand, face decisions that only the CEO can make. You make the critical decisions that drive business and deliver for customers and shareholders. You make decisions when data is unclear and the consequences and implications are unknown. These decisions are significantly harder and more impactful than any other you've had to make as an executive.

I knew all of this going into the job, but it didn't alleviate the pressure when I was the one actually making those decisions. Luckily, I had an amazing board at Art.com; no questions were dumb questions, and we discussed everything both in formal board meetings and in productive one-on-one conversations.

YPO's Role

I attended my first YPO event in May 2017, about six months after starting at Art.com. I joined my forum four months later.

My forum members helped me with all aspects of being a CEO, but over time, I came to appreciate the help the other members offered on topics that went beyond business. Just as I was supporting my company through its transformation, YPO was supporting me. YPO helped me understand that the better your physical and mental state, the better you are able to make decisions and handle stress at work.

I also learned how to better balance the demands of work with my role at home, which, as we all know, can be easier said than done. For example, our YPO chapter recently had an event with Dr. Madeline Levine, author of *The Price of Privilege.* She has just written another book called *Teach Your Children Well.* The book is about raising children of privilege when at least one parent is in a high-intensity role. Madeline talked about how we can be the best parent or partner while also being the best version of ourselves at work.

Making an Impact

Pretty much everyone in my first forum was new to YPO. Two people had been in YPO before, but the forum itself was new. Nevertheless, our first retreat was extraordinary. I was blown away by how willing everyone was to share their experiences and feelings. We got deep with one another. Although we were a group of highly accomplished people from different backgrounds, and we all were in charge of various businesses and facing our own professional and personal issues, we opened up to each other instantly.

That retreat was only the second time we had all been together, but it set the tone for how our forum would work in the future. We agreed our conversations would never be shallow or superficial. We would always strive to have meaningful interactions. We wanted to have a high impact on every person involved.

The forum wasn't something we felt obligated to participate in; it was and continues to be extremely important to each of us. We all wanted it to be highly valuable, and for that to happen, we needed to be vulnerable. We needed to go deep quite quickly.

It felt like we were all learning together. We all seemed to understand that the best way to have an extraordinary outcome personally and collectively is to give that experience your best. Nobody ever acted tired or appeared impatient to leave. We all had the same spirit of engagement.

The Whole Person

My career, while important to me, has not been the be-all and end-all of my life. I've wanted to sustain and grow a high-intensity career while also growing and maintaining a marriage, a family, and a community. I've also hoped to maintain a certain level of mental well-being and sanity!

This is no small challenge. But the more I got to know the YPO community, the more I realized that every member of the organization wants similar things. They all want to be a whole person—not just a successful CEO. What's more, everyone cares about what everyone else is going through. If something is vital to a member at a certain time, the same thing is vital to everyone.

#Upside

Becoming a CEO has been an extraordinary experience. Since joining Art.com, I have helped rebuild and diversify the leadership team. The leadership team is now half women and includes African Americans and Hispanic Americans. We've also rebuilt the engineering organization, and in July 2018, we relaunched the Art.com brand and reinvented the experience from top to bottom. We redesigned everything from the brand catalog and the homepage to the web experience and mobile app. Under the hood, we have re-platformed much of the Art.com online experience, including our search capabilities, and completely overhauled how we build and ship code.

One of the hashtags I use is #upside. When a company has been around for eighteen years, there's more upside with every turn.

YPO and my forum have been beside me throughout this

journey. First-time CEOs like me often struggle with gauging how many of their issues and concerns are normal. You encounter questions you never faced in other C-suite roles. When that happened to me, the YPO community was a valuable sounding board. It was a place where I could affirm that my feelings and concerns were normal. If something ever felt a little unusual, the community could help me think about it differently.

YPO fosters relationships that are different from any others I've had. Our YPO forums consist of a small group of people who are willing to have intimate conversations. That's why I feel very fortunate that I joined YPO early in my CEO journey. I never faced a time where I was stuck and didn't know whom to talk to.

I also appreciate examining the issues my forum mates bring up. When I was just starting out, I'd listen to their challenges and realize that I might be facing similar concerns within six months. That's why I love the monthly meetings with my forum: whenever we work through another member's issue together, I realize that the solution could someday help me.

Words of Encouragement

In all areas of life, you get out what you put in. I've had conversations with people who are unsure about joining YPO because they think they have no time. In reality, everyone's busy, especially the CEOs who are a part of YPO.

YPO is a commitment like any other. You are expected to be engaged and present in any meeting or event you attend.

In my experience, YPO forum meetings are some of the best hours of my month. Each session is refreshing and thoughtful, and it gives me foresight I wouldn't get on my own. YPO helps me see around corners I wouldn't otherwise see around. I've had the opportunity to tackle difficult, challenging, and unknown topics, whether personal or professional.

The commitment to YPO is an extremely good investment. It's an investment in yourself, your career, and your evolution in all facets of life.

CHAPTER THREE

Be an Upstander, Not a Bystander

Steven Aldrich, Chief Product Officer of GoDaddy

Steven joined GoDaddy in 2012 through the acquisition of the on-line bookkeeping service where he was CEO. Previous leadership experiences include being CEO of a brain-fitness gaming company, spending a decade at Intuit, and cofounding and leading an online service that simplified shopping for insurance.

AFTER A DECADE AT INTUIT, I DECIDED TO GET BACK INTO entrepreneurship. I wanted to push myself and use everything I had learned from the great leaders there about operating a business at scale. So, in the fall of 2008, I took a job as the CEO of a neuroscience startup in San Francisco that applied brain plasticity research to computer games.

One day in 2009, I ran into Mari Baker, whom I knew from Intuit. She said I should join YPO because it would help me build up my network in San Francisco and would be a great resource as I made the difficult decisions required of CEOs.

I was not new to the world of a CEO. I was the founder and CEO of an early e-commerce startup in the mid-1990s in Alexandria, Virginia. Someone suggested then that I join YPO, but at the time, it didn't occur to me that there were things I didn't know, so I never pursued the idea. I had recently graduated from Stanford with an MBA, where a professor had encouraged me to take a business plan I had written for his class for an online insurance marketplace and start the company. I was so busy building the business that all I could focus on were the day-to-day decisions, partnerships, recruiting, selling, and developing the technology we needed. I did not make the time for YPO as I did not appreciate how I could benefit.

In fact, the only time I remember feeling nervous during my first stint as a CEO was when we hired a computer scientist from Penn State. His name was Zhu, and he and his family moved down from Happy Valley, Pennsylvania, to join the company. I remember feeling a little nervous at that point; Zhu had picked up and left his PhD program to work with us, and I felt pressure to ensure that things worked out. I remember telling my wife that the company had to succeed now because someone with a family had put his faith in us.

When I sold that company to Intuit and came into contact with Intuit's spectacular leaders, it became obvious that I didn't have enough losses under my belt to understand how much I still had to learn. Suddenly, I was surrounded by people with much more experience than I had in a variety of areas—from performance reviews to process excellence, decision-making processes, and scaling leadership across thousands of people.

In business, as in life, judgment is informed by experience. As a first-time CEO, I didn't have enough experience to know what I did not know. I would say that I was unconsciously incompetent.

However, by the time I met Mari in the city ten years later, I had a healthy dose of life experience. When I started leading the San Francisco-based neuroscience company in 2008, I expected we would be in growth mode. Three weeks after I arrived, the Great Recession hit, and that focus on growth quickly shifted to a focus on survival. Maximum effort was required from the entire team. To get through that period and build a sustainable business model, the organization had to be cut down by 90 percent. The effort required *a lot* of energy and a new business model that could work with far fewer people.

So when Mari suggested YPO, my attitude about what I knew and what I still needed to learn had changed. Getting outside perspective from fellow leaders who were neither board members nor family sounded like an opportunity to help me clear the fog and keep perspective.

That moment seemed like the right time to join YPO.

Clearing the Fog

It was a relief to have a group of people with whom I could talk about what was happening. I could discuss the decisions I needed to make without wondering if the objectives of my listeners were aligned with mine. I spent a lot of time discussing my business, but I also had conversations about my own mental and physical well-being.

When you choose to be a CEO, you also choose to make sacrifices. The most significant sacrifice was that I couldn't spend as much time with my family as I would have liked. I spoke about this with my wife, Allison, and my eight-year-old son, Jackson, before taking the role, explaining that being a CEO in San Francisco (an hour-plus commute from home) meant leaving when it was dark and returning when it was dark every day. I would also miss plenty of nights and weekends by traveling and working, which meant missed opportunities, such as being unable to coach youth sports.

YPO offered the opportunity to talk through all the facets of that time with my peers. My forum helped me clear the fog around my decisions. I discussed eliminating the field sales-force, building compelling games, and finding alternative ways to finance the spectacular scientists we didn't want to lose. Talking through the decisions gave me a chance to structure my thinking, get multiple perspectives, and weigh my options without judgment. While I had gotten the firm to cash-flow positive, I questioned whether I was enjoying what I was doing and if the role was the best fit for my skill set. Ultimately, I went to the board with the recommendation that we make one of my direct reports the CEO. He was a neuroscientist by training and also had tremendous business acumen, and he continues to do a great job leading the business. We also restructured the equity ownership to give the employees more incentives to stay and grow the company. I left excited to spend more time with Allison and Jackson and think through what was next.

Fairness and Equity

While YPO was helping to sharpen my actions, an experience with Mari Baker honed my feelings about what it means to have a fair and transparent workplace.

Mari was a Stanford trustee, and she had invited me to be her guest at an event honoring benefactors of Stanford Hospital, where several of the neuroscience researchers would present their work.

I was not prepared for what happened at the event. Every person we met assumed that I, and not Mari, was one of the donors being honored. As each person thanked me for my donation, I repeatedly explained that Mari was the donor and I was attending the event as her guest. It was embarrassing, and I spent the entire night apologizing to Mari.

She explained to me that this sort of thing happened all the time; it was an unconscious bias people shared. But it was new to me. Seeing the obvious outcomes coming from unconscious bias shocked me.

That event made it crystal clear that assumptions and biases were preventing accomplished people from thinking Mari could have been the donor. I started to look for ways in which people's assumptions and biases got in the way in other parts of life as well.

Putting Change into Action

That evening's experience exposed the need for me to be more vocal and public about explicit and unconscious bias. After leaving the neuroscience company, I found my next role as the CEO of Outright, an online bookkeeping service. I had the opportunity to build a leadership team where 50 percent of my direct reports were women. This new group of leaders came together as a high-performing team, growing engaged users tremendously as e-commerce marketplaces such as Etsy, Amazon, and eBay generated data that we turned into organized insights for customers. That success led to GoDaddy's acquisition of Outright in 2012 to seed its first California office.

When I joined, GoDaddy had a polarizing external reputation

based on its Super Bowl advertising from the 2000s. Founded in 1999, the company had become the largest provider of domain names, websites, and hosting services, and it was focused on leveling the playing field for millions of everyday entrepreneurs. The company helps people with ideas look great and grow their business online by providing affordable access to technology and people. As we added new leaders and combined with the existing team, the group embraced the concept of leveling the playing field not just for our customers but also for our employees. I didn't want to be a bystander, a term I learned from my son's elementary school, and go with the flow. Instead, I wanted to be an *upstander* and drive change. What I needed, along with the rest of the organization, was a toolkit to apply to the problem.

GoDaddy's approach to ensuring equitable treatment for all employees started at the top with CEO Blake Irving, who set the tone after he joined in 2013. The vision was to recruit the best talent we could and retain that talent by giving every person the same chance to work on exciting projects and get promoted. He made it a priority with the leadership team, our people ops group, and the Clayman Institute for Gender Research at Stanford to explain our objectives, create best practices, and collect and share data on how we were doing.

The Clayman institute's data-driven approach was grounded in research about the causes and effects of bias. Their help was crucial in helping us create a gender-blind process in all the components of day-to-day work. I shared interview guides and performance reviews I had written with the Institute's research team as part of the effort to review our forms and the way in which our feedback was provided. We looked at pay by job type and gender, promotions by level and gender, and the processes and artifacts involved in those decisions. The review process was thorough, and that level of detail was critical to building a systemic approach to ensure everyone in the workplace had a chance to succeed.

For example, we rewrote our job descriptions to characterize jobs in unbiased ways, removing expressions such as "rock star coder" that stereotype who can be a great developer. The more we focused on creating objective job descriptions and participated in events such as the Grace Hopper Conference, the more we found ourselves hiring women for new engineering jobs. The increase in the number of women coming directly out of undergraduate programs was so significant that we are now closing in on a fifty-fifty split between male and female interns. Previously, those positions were predominantly filled by males.

While we made a conscious effort to include and hire more women, our goal was to make our practices better for everybody. By applying consistent best practices, we saw a significant increase in the quality of feedback given to all of our employees, and the amount of time it takes to get promoted from first-level engineer to second-level engineer became more uniform. This all happened because we were much more focused on equality, which benefited everybody.

To make wholesale change in a company, you must enlist everybody and give them a reason to support a new approach. A CEO can't solely focus on one group's benefit without telling the rest of the organization why the change would benefit them also. Creating a clear and consistent set of standards—and ensuring they are applied everywhere—creates a workplace where the best performers are rewarded, regardless of gender, race, or "style."

In this case, it was essential for everyone to understand that without a fair set of processes, hiring standards, and pay standards, the company would get it wrong for lots of people. Everyone wants an environment where each person is judged by the same standards. Everyone wants a fair and unbiased environment that creates better outcomes for customers. Instead of pitting one group against another, my approach is to allow everyone to get on board and be part of the solution.

Law of Attraction

I once read a study in which researchers concluded that you can tell whether a person will have healthy habits by looking at their friends. The people you know are great predictors of your behavior.

By this logic, a group of successful leaders who are curious and want to learn and improve will attract like-minded people. This has been the case for YPO. My Golden Gate chapter has attracted talented and curious members who want to drive change. Every member believes that if something isn't working, they'll try to fix it.

The monthly meetings of the chapter have brought me in touch with members' interests, including charter schools, the state police, the opera, caring for aging parents, nonprofits focused on healthy and affordable meals for kids, internet access in schools, prison reform, and community service.

Since joining YPO in 2009, my forum meetings have been an essential sounding board for major decisions. When I decided to leave the neuroscience company, my forum members helped me determine the best way to approach the situation. When I was the CEO of Outright, I got valuable input about options to fuel our growth, and one of the forum members told me that GoDaddy was looking to create an office in Silicon Valley and made the introduction to the company's investors. If not for his introduction, that acquisition might never have come about.

YPO's influence on the social side of my life has also been meaningful. One example was a trip to the 2012 Olympics in London organized by a member of our YPO chapter. We went as a family with a group of other chapter members and had an amazing time. That was a once-in-a-lifetime experience and created memories that are still fresh of seeing Usain Bolt, Mo Farah, and the US women's national soccer team win gold medals.

Being part of YPO has extended beyond the local chapter to a global reach. Through another YPO chapter, I was able twice to be a part of the US Navy's Distinguished Visitor Embark Program, once spending a day on a nuclear aircraft carrier and another time going deep on a nuclear submarine. The size and purpose of these two ships are obvious, but the scale differences hit home for me through the experience: there were more than 5,000 people on the carrier (including the sailors and the air wing) and fewer than a hundred on the submarine. It was eye-opening to learn how differently these organizations are run and the distinctive approach each takes in selecting and training the sailors. A clear example is that on the aircraft carrier, there are multiple people for each job, while on the submarine, each person learns multiple jobs. I came back with an appreciation of the impact these machines could have, the determination to build them, and the ability to figure out the right organizational model to get the most out of the crew. Those observations gave me another piece of evidence that there is no right way to organize a team, and instead there is the best way to structure the people I have for the objectives and situation we are facing.

Impact

My forum helps me talk through the good and bad things that happen outside of work, such as my volunteer role with a local glass arts nonprofit group. I have headed the board for the Bay Area Glass Institute (BAGI) for over fifteen years, and the organization has had many ups and downs. As head of the board, there are times when I want external input on decisions about the direction and my leadership of the organization. YPO fills that role for me.

My forum mates hold me accountable to making changes to that organization to improve its impact on the community. I am excited about where BAGI is today compared to where it was when I first joined YPO, and I don't think those changes would have happened without my YPO peers' insight. YPO helped me make some difficult decisions that have made the organization more effective.

When I joined YPO, I had been a leader in the corporate world for almost twenty years. I knew the world was changing, that I was changing, and that I would still benefit from help and input along the way. Thanks to YPO, I have the chance to clear the fog that obscures potential solutions and, in talking through others' circumstances, learn lessons I can apply back to my own life. One day a month, I meet with people who assist me through making better decisions—decisions that can have enormous implications on my business and my personal life.

At the time I joined, YPO seemed worth the investment. Now that I look back, I can confirm it has been.

CHAPTER FOUR

Paying It Forward

Leah Solivan, Founder of TaskRabbit

A vision for revolutionizing the way people work led Leah to pioneer the concept of service networking. Her passion for product innovation and devotion to user experience has propelled TaskRabbit into a leading role in the collaborative consumption movement.

Since bootstrapping TaskRabbit in 2008, Leah has expanded the company nationally, grown the team to more than sixty employees, and raised nearly $40 million in venture funding from well-known investors such as Shasta Ventures, Lightspeed Venture Partners, and Founders Fund. TaskRabbit has also inspired legions of startups to launch in the collaborative and service-networking space.

Fast Company named Leah one of the 100 Most Creative People in Business, and her achievements have been featured in the Wall Street Journal, Wired, *and* Time.

In 2014, Leah was inaugurated into the Forum of Young Global Leaders, a prestigious group of fewer than 1,000 people around the globe recognized for their bold, brave, action-oriented entre-

preneurial ventures that are having a global impact. As a Latina,
she is passionate about bringing diversity to business culture and
also enjoys speaking on topics related to the future of work, women
in technology, and entrepreneurship. She has facilitated workshops
and delivered speeches around the globe, including at the World
Economic Forum in Davos, Switzerland, the University of Oxford
in the UK, and Tina Brown's Women in the World Summit in
New York City.

I INITIALLY HEARD ABOUT YPO A FEW YEARS AFTER I'D
started TaskRabbit. At the time, TaskRabbit was still in the
growth stage. I had raised a few rounds of funding, and we had
a team of about fifty people and were in about fifteen markets in the United States. Running the company took a lot of
time and hard work. What's more, I was eight months pregnant.
Anything new in my life had to be valuable, because I had a lot
of things competing for my time.

Mari Baker introduced me to YPO thinking I would get a lot out
of the organization. A few weeks later, she came by the Task-
Rabbit offices to talk more about YPO with me.

I was intrigued. I didn't have a lot of background in business—
before founding TaskRabbit and becoming its CEO, I was an
engineer at IBM for eight years—so the idea of having a group
of CEOs as mentors and confidants appealed to me. I talked
with Mari at length about the organization, and I spoke with
other members of the Golden Gate chapter as well. I wanted to
hear about as many of their experiences with YPO as I could
so I could gauge whether joining the organization would be
helpful for me.

I knew how lonely the job of CEO can be. I was twenty-eight

when I founded TaskRabbit, and I didn't have a lot of peers who could relate to my situation and the pressures I faced.

I ultimately joined YPO for the opportunity to learn from other CEOs who knew how to scale and sell their businesses. But I also liked how the confidential forums helped members feel comfortable talking about their personal life and family. YPO would allow me to empathize with others and receive the same empathy in return. That side of the organization was compelling, and I realized I might not be able to get that support anywhere else.

Light in a Dark Box

Just as I had hoped it would, my forum helps me gain perspective and insight. As a founder of a business, I often feel as if I'm living in a dark box. I can't see anything inside. I try and feel my way around in the darkness and get a grasp of what's in front of me.

My YPO forum shines light into that box. Every conversation pokes a new hole and allows glimpses of sunlight that help me distinguish the world around me.

The other members often see situations differently than I do, but they also know me well enough to tie each situation into my history and context. I find every piece of feedback I receive to be so valuable. Even though someone's perspective might be different from my own, I appreciate that all the feedback I get is grounded and has context behind it.

Tricky Transitions

Eight years after starting TaskRabbit, I decided to transition from CEO to chairwoman of the board. While I loved founding the company and building it up, after eight years, TaskRabbit had changed dramatically. It was at a different stage in size and scale, and I was often nostalgic for the early stages of the business, when it had just been me and a close team of ten or twenty people building, innovating, and figuring out the company's game plan.

While I spent years thinking about that decision, I didn't pull the trigger until I talked about it with my forum and other members of YPO over several months. YPO helped me realize that those early stages are where my passions lie. These conversations made me confident that the transition was right for personal and professional reasons.

At the time, I was also pregnant with my second child. When I had my first child two and half years earlier, I didn't get any time off because of the business, and I was dreading the thought of going through that kind of intensity again. I also realized that the company didn't need me to run myself into the ground. At this point, it was the perfect opportunity to transition from CEO to chairwoman.

The transition was surprisingly smooth. In the time I'd run TaskRabbit, I had built a strong team around me. I had recruited Stacy Brown-Philpot from Google to be my COO, and she had been doing fantastic work for four years.

After discussing the transition with my forum, the first person I spoke to was Stacy. We had already talked a lot about our own personal goals, so she knew where my passions lie, and I knew that she had a dream of being a CEO of a mid- to late-stage company.

The transition felt organic, seamless, and comfortable. Everything felt right. Thanks to YPO, my forum, and Stacy, I was
confident about the decision I was making. Not only did I trust
Stacy, but the rest of the team trusted her, too. What's more,
I didn't face the challenge of bringing in an outsider who might
not understand the business, the team, or the culture.

As soon as Stacy became CEO of the company, I encouraged
her to join YPO. I told her it would be great for her and would
create future success for the business. Stacy is now part of the
Barbary Coast chapter in the Bay Area.

Everything came full circle.

Following the transition, I became executive chairwoman of
the board, which allowed me to stay plugged in and participate
in executive-level conversations. I made a conscious effort to
support Stacy and help her fill whatever gaps emerged. If she
needed a little empathy or someone to vent to, I would be there.

Stacy and I quickly became comfortable in our new roles. I had
already been running the TaskRabbit board meetings for the
last seven years, and I had also been a member of both a nonprofit board—at my alma mater, Sweet Briar College—and a
private company called Galvanize. These experiences gave me
perspective on how to be a successful executive chairwoman.

As my due date approached, we were able to wind down my
involvement in the day-to-day operations of the company.
That year, I was able to take a real leave, which I desperately
wanted. That was a profound feeling and gave me a sense of
accomplishment.

The Sale of TaskRabbit

Stepping aside as CEO was not my last big transition with Task-Rabbit. Just as the company was about to turn ten, we decided to sell it.

I was ready for the business to continue to grow and flourish beyond me. While I can't speak for all founders, I suspect most of us aim to create a successful business that can live beyond us. I am proud that we were able to reach that level of success with TaskRabbit.

The sale posed many logistical, economic, and emotional challenges, but YPO was right there with me throughout. I talked with my forum and other YPO members about the sale for nine to twelve months before it actually happened, and it was crucial to have the perspective of others who had sold their companies before. The emotional aspect of selling the business was easier because I had already transitioned out of the CEO role and let go of a lot of the day-to-day control of the company.

By finding a strategic partner like IKEA, TaskRabbit could continue to grow and flourish beyond what I had created. The partnership with IKEA would also turn TaskRabbit into a globally recognized brand. More importantly, IKEA and TaskRabbit both emphasized sustainability, people, and driving success at work. This alignment around values and culture was compelling.

Even though I have two beautiful kids, Amelia and Ryan, Task-Rabbit will always be my first baby. When I sold the business, I felt like I was sending my first kid off to college. I had prepared them well for what they would face without me, and now it was time to let go.

The Next Step

The sale of TaskRabbit left me facing a significant question: what should I do next? I had spent eight years as an engineer at IBM, followed by almost a decade of running my own company. Whatever I did next, I knew I wanted to dedicate a decade and beyond to it, so I homed in on venture. Venture is a long-term commitment—funds have a ten-year return cycle—and would allow me to stay at the forefront of the tech industry. Because I am an engineer by training, I love being at the forefront of emerging technologies. Venture gives me the opportunity for continuous learning—everything from artificial intelligence and virtual reality to the blockchain and other technologies I'd missed out on while I was running my company. I knew I didn't want to put my head down in a single technology or business again, and venture would give me the privilege of continually learning and exploring.

But which firm? How big and at what stage?

Although my gut was pulling me toward a firm in its early stages, I still tried out Series A funds, growth funds, and late-stage funds so I could learn the overall venture landscape. Ultimately, early-stage investing resonated with me the most. I loved my early-stage experience at TaskRabbit and was keen to meet with founders in that same position.

Around that time, I met my future business partner, Chris Howard, and decided to join Chris's Fuel Capital as a general partner. Chris and I had never crossed paths before, but we had mutual friends. Investing in and working with founders made me still feel like an entrepreneur, and Fuel gave me the opportunity to join an emerging fund and help build it up over time. I couldn't pass up such a compelling opportunity.

Today, I'm a general partner at Fuel Capital, which is still an early-stage venture fund. We are investing out of a $46 million fund and getting involved with the earliest stages of a company. I love working with companies when they're just starting with a couple of founders and an idea. My favorite time at TaskRabbit was when we had fewer than ten people.

Investing in future companies and helping entrepreneurs build their dream businesses drives my passions. Even if we don't ultimately invest in a company, I love sitting down with a founder and hearing their story. That pleasure comes from having walked in their shoes. I understand the kind of decisions they're making. I have an idea of what's keeping them up at night. Having that empathy helps me be a better investor.

Giving Back

While I have been a member of YPO for many years, I recently joined the Officers Team so I could help integrate new members. The Officers Team also allows me to get to know people in a smaller group setting, which I love.

I also began running the membership for our chapter, which allows me to give back. YPO helped me through significant transitions, and I want other founders, entrepreneurs, and CEOs to receive the same benefits. I especially want to help entrepreneurs who might not otherwise have support or who are part of underrepresented communities.

Most people considering YPO are concerned about the time it requires. YPO *is* a time commitment. If you're part of a forum, you have to commit half a day a month. That is a lot for anyone, especially a CEO or a working parent, but being able to share stories and experiences through YPO usually gets people over that hump. Almost everyone commits after they speak to a YPO member and learn the value of the organization.

I am thankful to the women—such as Mari Baker, Megan Gardner, Cara France, and others—who served in leadership and chaired the chapter before me. I look forward to chairing the chapter myself, hoping to inspire both men and women to learn and grow, just as I have through my own personal YPO journey. I am grateful for the opportunity to continue to contribute to the organization. An adage from YPO is *you get out of YPO what you put in.* I am my own biggest beneficiary of the volunteer work I do. Leading CEOs, men and women alike, is a learning experience like no other.

CHAPTER FIVE

A Little Advice Goes a Long Way

Chris O'Neill, CEO of Evernote

Chris is a technology industry leader with decades of experience building and growing successful products, brands, and teams. As CEO of Evernote, he is turning a beloved, globally recognized brand into a productivity powerhouse beyond its already sizable 220-million-member base. Chris is a strategic and masterful team builder, athlete, angel investor, husband, and father. He loves Evernote because it helps people and teams remember everything, turn ideas into action, and work effortlessly together.

I WAS WORKING AT GOOGLE IN CALIFORNIA WHEN I FIRST learned about YPO. From time to time, we would give YPO members a tour of the Google campus. Although I was intrigued by the group, I wasn't in a position to join, so I filed the idea away as something to reconsider at some point down the road.

I moved to Canada to head up Google's operations there. Sometime during my first year in Canada, a man named Shaun Francis tracked me down and invited me to breakfast. Shaun, the chair and CEO of Medcan and one of a select group of Canadians ever to graduate from the US Naval Academy, told me all about YPO and encouraged me to join. It sounded fascinating, but I told Shaun I was still getting up to speed with my new role and needed to wait.

I stayed in touch with Shaun, however, and soon met another guy, Daniel Debow, the CEO and co-founder of Helpful.com. Daniel also urged me to join YPO. Frankly, I had my doubts about YPO. I was incredibly busy at that time, and I wasn't sure how much I would actually get out of the organization. I certainly didn't feel the need to have more social engagements.

But in 2011, I joined the forum that Shaun and Daniel were in. At the time, it was called the Ontario chapter, but today, it's known as the Maple Leaf chapter. My primary reason for joining was my forum mates, particularly Daniel. He is also in the tech industry, and he helped me realize that I was thinking about YPO too narrowly. I thought the organization was primarily focused on professional connections and development, but Daniel persuaded me that YPO also provided its members with a holistic perspective on life. It was a chance to develop as a person. There was an element of socialization through retreats, he said, but the underlying value is to help you learn and develop in all aspects of life.

Ultimately, this is exactly what happened.

Time to Reflect

As you go through life, you develop a sense that the more you learn, the less you know. This is what happened to me.

Although I'm originally from Canada, moving back there for this new job was a challenge. I had declined other offers to manage Google Canada, and when I finally accepted, I was convinced that it would be a great move for my family and me. My wife was not so sure at first—she was born and raised in California and Atlanta, Georgia, and she didn't love the idea of leaving our great life in California and moving up to Canada. Eventually, I persuaded her. That summer, we hustled to get our kids, pets, cars, and stuff across the border and settled in time for our son to start kindergarten. It was chaotic.

Also challenging was the fact that this was my first time in a senior position. I was the lead person in the country for Google Canada. My official title was managing director of Google Canada, which meant that when the government was unhappy with Google, I was the person they'd call. Once a quarter, my counterpart in engineering and I would present to Google's CEO and his team.

I experienced the loneliness often associated with CEOs. I had a high-profile role in a high-profile company. There was a lot that I needed help with. While I had an amazing wife and beautiful young kids, I didn't feel like I could go to them with all my dilemmas. Similarly, there were some things I didn't want to talk to my boss about.

YPO was an opportunity for me to relate to others in a safe, trusted environment without an angle or agenda. I believe it's important to talk to and connect with people who have been in a similar situation, and YPO allowed me to do that. YPO was a great way to get an objective perspective on the things that were going on in my life.

YPO also gave me the necessary time to reflect. In our chaotic lives, we are all so overwhelmed with information. We are bombarded with emails, texts, and Slack messages. It's necessary to put that stuff aside once in a while and reflect on all aspects of our lives.

Making Moves

We moved to Canada when I was thirty-eight, and our first two years there were hugely successful. Our business more than doubled, going from a $600 million startup to a $2 billion business in three to four years. We were recognized as Canada's best and most innovative brand, and as the Best Place to Work each year I was there.

Although the tech industry in Canada was thriving, my gut told me that if I wanted to stay in the tech industry, I needed to move back to the Bay Area. In Canada, I was a big fish in a relatively small pond. Some people enjoy that feeling, but I like to be a small fish in a big pond.

So after I turned forty-two, we packed up and moved back to California. I started pursuing more esoteric parts of Google by joining the Moonshot Factory, a part of Google X. Imagine an office of Peter Pan types running around with childlike curiosity about everything in the world. That was Google X. The people there ask big questions about levitation and self-driving cars and balloons that can provide internet in times of crisis. In the year I spent there, I worked on the intersection of wearable technology at Google, such as Google Glass, and looking for ways to build promising technologies into businesses.

Google X was such a crazy and wonderful collection of people. If I moved twenty meters in any direction, I'd find a person who was world class at something. I see this as one of the most surprising, fascinating, and dysfunctional times of my professional life.

Although Google was a profound experience, I got to the point where I felt like my learning curve was starting to flatten out. I was learning marvelous things, getting exposure, and having great experiences, but I was also craving something more. I like to continually challenge myself to learn as much as I can in life.

I also missed the autonomy I'd enjoyed in Canada. In the context of a large company like Google, Canada was big enough to matter but small enough that nobody really cared. This sense of autonomy had become more important to me than I realized.

Around this time, Sequoia Capital approached me about some opportunities within its portfolio. Evernote was one of them. I met with the board, and the more I learned about Evernote, the more interested I became. The opportunity reminded me of the sort of autonomy I'd had in Canada.

I also connected with Evernote as a user and felt I could make a difference working there; I had begun using the product during our move to Canada, when there were so many things to keep track of. I wanted to learn, but I also wanted to work on products and brands that I could connect with on a deeper level. I wanted to make a difference.

Jumping in at Evernote

Every business has a startup phase in which you think about why you exist and how a product fits into a market. In a startup phase, a business decides whether it's viable. The next step is the scale-up phase, when a company is expanding its processes, from supporting customers to sales marketing to engineering and product. Very few companies make it past the startup phase. Fewer still figure out the scale-up phase.

Both Google and Evernote were past their startup phases when I joined. As businesses, there was a lot they had figured out. But Evernote struggled through its scale-up phase.

Evernote is based on the visionary work of its founder, Stepan Pachikov. About eighteen years ago, Pachikov decided there was too much information coming at him, from Spanish poetry to computer science to photography. He wanted a digital extension of his brain to store it all, so he began to develop what became Evernote.

Evernote burst on the scene and was revolutionary for its time. Pachikov brought together a strong team, and the company took advantage of the world's different platforms, from a computer to a smartphone to the web. The app store gave Evernote global distribution, and the Cloud revolution helped even more.

Evernote's success is one part serendipity, one part the genius of Pachikov, and one part the genius of the team. Together, these parts put Evernote on the map as a category leader.

Back to YPO

I rejoined YPO in September 2016, about a year after starting at Evernote. I assumed it would be easy to transfer from the Maple Leaf chapter to the Golden Gate one, but I had to start from scratch. This is just another way of ensuring the organization maintains a high-quality standard.

My second time through, I saw the process through different eyes. There's a sense of mystery about the YPO application process, and while the experience is exciting, it's also a little daunting the first time around. When I reapplied for YPO in California, I already had real experiences to draw from.

After joining the Golden Gate chapter, I quickly realized how much variety the Bay Area group had. It wasn't all tech, as I'd assumed it would be, but included many different industry groups.

Industry Diversity

Many of us experience similar opportunities and challenges in life. While we all walk different paths and come from different places, we still all wrestle with many of the same issues.

Speaking to experts from different industries at YPO often gives me a fresh perspective. Sometimes you can get so close to a tree that your nose gets stuck on the sap. When you take a step back, you get a new perspective. You might actually be able to see a way forward. The more diversity there is in a group of people, the more you can see through the fog of an issue.

YPO also helps keep me grounded in the high-stakes world of Silicon Valley. In the Bay Area, even when your business is performing well by any objective standard, you may not feel like you're doing well enough because the expectations are so high.

People in my YPO forum sometimes ask me how I would think about my issue if I were anywhere but the Bay Area. How would I think about the problem? How would I think about the opportunity? How would I think about that discussion? The truth is that if I weren't in the Bay Area, I would probably be much happier and more satisfied with my work and our company's success. Changing your perspective and imagining how you'd feel doing business somewhere else can be reassuring and re-store your sense of what's real and what's distorted by the tight, high-stakes world around you. Suddenly, your issue doesn't seem so crucial, and your company's growth rate doesn't ap-pear so bad. These discussions give you a healthier outlook on what's happening.

YPO helps me navigate the big issues as well as the little ones. It's inevitable that any CEO will make mistakes, but a good CEO will avoid the big ones and learn from every setback and mis-take. Whether you are trying to decide how to structure your board or how to compensate executives, YPO can help. Some of these issues might seem like small, mundane examples, but cumulatively, they make a big difference.

While YPO probably isn't the only place a CEO can turn, it's a remarkable organization in its responsiveness and objectivity. Throughout the CEO journey, it's vital to get help in both big and small ways.

A Good Leader

In those big moments—like when you are thinking about rais-ing money or making a big hire or fire—having someone there to point out your blind spots is invaluable. One of the loneliest parts of being a CEO is that people don't always tell you what you need to hear. YPO fills that gap.

When it comes to juggling life's demands, no one ever gets it right, including me. But I love having perspective on the ebb and flow of life. I love hearing about and learning from others' experiences. YPO gives me this.

I strive to honor the commitments I make to myself and others, so I value having the chance to make those commitments at YPO and then be held accountable. Just as I am comfortable reflecting on my achievements, I feel comfortable reflecting on where I fall short. YPO gives me that opportunity.

A leader must be able to absorb criticism, especially when things go wrong. When the opposite happens and a company achieves a milestone, a leader should distribute the credit. A CEO's job is simultaneously to absorb criticism and distribute credit.

As humans, we tend to absorb the stress that surrounds us. When this happens to me, I think of the adage *you're half as good and half as bad as you think you are.* At YPO, you are surrounded by people who can provide objective feedback and observation, as well as shine light on both the bad and the good.

CHAPTER SIX

Navigating a New World

Lily Sarafan, CEO of Home Care Assistance

Lily is president and CEO of Home Care Assistance, which provides products and services that enable happy, healthy aging at home. She has led the company from startup to sector leader with more than 7,000 employees across 170 markets. HCA is consistently recognized as a best-in-class consumer service, and Lily is a featured expert on innovation in healthcare and the future of aging.

Lily is also a board member, investor, and advisor for innovative companies, including genetic screening pioneer Counsyl. Her board service extends to high-impact nonprofits, including the Stanford Alumni Association, The Freeman Spogli Institute for International Studies, the AMENA center for Building Innovation Economies, and The Women's Alzheimer's Movement. She is a founding partner of Project BIG: The Stanford Brain Immune Gut Initiative and serves in various leadership roles to advance civil society, global economic development, and precision health. For her leadership at the helm of a healthcare industry champion, she has been named

Ernst & Young Entrepreneur of the Year, Women Health Care Executives Woman of the Year, World Economic Forum Young Global Leader, and a Silicon Valley 40 Under 40.

YPO WAS ON MY RADAR LONG BEFORE I JOINED. WHETHER it's at a Stanford board or council meeting, at a healthcare conference, or at The Aspen Institute, YPO comes up in conversation fondly and often. The organization has an impeccable reputation for connecting leaders and allowing them to leverage shared knowledge and form lasting friendships.

In 2016, I was referred to the membership coordinator of the Golden Gate chapter. Although I deeply admired my peers who spoke so highly of YPO, I was reluctant to join at first because I wasn't sure I had the bandwidth to fully commit. Then a friend of mine told me that joining YPO would actually *expand* my capacity rather than impede it.

After that, I met with two or three active chapter members. These individuals were as committed in their lives as I was, if not more so, and I quickly understood the value they ascribed to the organization. Soon after, I went to a membership meeting, which officially began my YPO journey.

The Value of Variety

The year 2015 marked the inflection point that inspired me to join YPO the following year. My company, Home Care Assistance (HCA), had grown to become the leading private pay provider of in-home care for seniors, and we were rapidly expanding our scope and scale, which would eventually result in a tripling of the organization over the next few years.

I was also involved in many political campaigns, Stanford initiatives, community engagements, and corporate and non-profit boards. I have an extensive set of interests, and I tend to dive deeply into anything I care about and advance the cause through leadership and innovation. Clearly, I had to carefully prioritize all of these interests. I was also eager to find others who were committed to a broad set of priorities and from whom I could learn about devoting energy successfully across an expansive set of activities.

Enter YPO, where I was granted an opportunity to interact with multifaceted CEOs across different sectors. These inter-actions were far more engaging and valuable than attending siloed industry conferences or networking events.

CEOs can talk to one another about anything from managing board relationships to refining digital marketing. I speak to my peers about when to maintain a lower profile and when to win the PR battle. These topics are fairly universal among organi-zation leaders, each of whom lends a unique perspective and set of experiences.

Regardless of the specific product or service, CEOs have to deal with the challenges of managing complex, living organizations. This involves retaining strong talent, delegating across remote teams, launching new products or initiatives, and exploring the opportunities associated with more sophisticated analytics and machine intelligence. Many CEOs also must handle legal issues, satisfy a growing constituency of stakeholders, custom-ers, and employees, and figure out how to navigate changes in the regulatory landscape.

I've benefited tremendously from interacting with other CEOs, not only in my forum but also across the chapter. I love having the opportunity to speak with YPO members who have a strong thesis about a particular subject and to find through our conversations the intersecting ideas that elevate our thinking and crystallize our plans.

The longer you've been affiliated with any organization, the harder it is to see outside perspectives and recognize nuances. YPO helps you step outside your world for a time and see your organization and life with fresh eyes.

The CEO's Challenges

YPO also helps manage the enormous responsibility and change CEOs face every day.

When HCA was a startup, I was involved in all areas of the business. In the early years of the company, I did everything from writing operations manuals to figuring out training, software systems, and how best to capture client data.

Since then, my day-to-day role has morphed. I divide my time more evenly between outlining our company's vision and strengthening our leadership teams to ensure we have the highest caliber talent. I also make sure we keep our finger on the pulse of the innovation happening around us in Silicon Valley and in the other regions where we have a presence.

When someone becomes a CEO after serving in many different companies, they can sense the gravity and scope of the role they've taken on. When a company grows around you from a fledgling startup, as ours did, there comes a time when you look around and wonder how it all happened. You feel like you're still sitting around a Formica table sketching out plans in a notebook, but in truth, you have thousands of team members now and are shifting the paradigm in your space.

Given how disciplined, competitive, and humble my team is, I've been more apt to recognize these vast changes from an external vantage point. For example, I've had the opportunity to participate in the once-a-decade White House Conference on Aging and contribute to public policy solutions. As a Scientific Advisory Board member of Maria Shriver's Women's Alzheimer's Movement, among other related roles, I've had the privilege of working to advance clinical research and consumer education on brain health and Alzheimer's disease, the most taxing and expensive disease in US history. These milestones make me grateful for all we've achieved and how our company continues to succeed and improve the human condition.

I have been a team leader most of my life, and my experience as an investor and mentor helps me advise the startup CEOs around me. Sometimes in the valley, we forget that the goal most often is to lead a company from startup to sustainable organization. There is so much excitement and hype around startups and fund-raising that we risk celebrating and reinforcing the wrong wins in this ecosystem. My YPO family serves a vital role in making sure we stay grounded, identify what's real, and always use a pragmatic lens to view our responsibilities and relationships.

How YPO Helps

At YPO, we talk about a wide variety of company-related topics—from title inflation to the power of data collection. One of the challenges we've discussed is how to enlist leaders from outside the company to take over roles held by others when the company was smaller. Not only are these outside leaders more experienced, but they're also coming into the organization with a more seasoned palate. As a leader, you want to make sure that original members of your team are in roles that are appropriate for where the company is in its current state. Consequently, I have benefited from others' insights on how to manage some of these transitions, which can be complex and far-reaching in their impact.

We have also discussed data integrity and how there needs to be consistency and discipline. This can be difficult because individual team members might have different interpretations of what it means to be well relative to baseline; for instance, some longitudinal trends in overall wellness aren't as precise as biomarkers might be.

YPO members have also taught me about confronting and engaging changes in the regulatory landscape, and we've talked about the right balance between asking for forgiveness and asking for permission.

I love that my whole self is not only welcome but also expected in a YPO discussion. In some professional settings, it's unusual for people to talk about their families, health issues, parents, or kids. This is not the case at YPO. When you bring those topics into a conversation, it becomes much more of an integrative experience. You get a holistic sense of a person's life story and the impact they want to make on the world.

There's much more to people than their primary career. Nowadays, more and more of us derive meaning and fulfillment from several different channels and pursuits. I see the beauty in the intersection of seemingly disparate areas or disciplines. These kinds of connections can be key to building and leading a world-class organization and leading a life of purpose and contentment.

Only Human

I'm a CEO, but that's not my only defining role. In YPO, I am surrounded by individuals who have a much broader set of intentions and engagements than those related solely to their companies.

Our society's expectations for institutional leaders are also changing. In the past, people didn't expect university presidents or corporate executives to take positions on social or political issues. If anything, people might be offended or confused if leaders were to take a stance.

When I was growing up, I was advised to keep my head down and focus on one or two things at a time because "you can't chase two rabbits at once." This is a parochial view. It presumes a universal, monolithic path for highly distinctive individuals and dismisses the alternative blueprints set forth by those leaders and learners who evoke more of a Renaissance spirit. In any case, what is expected of leaders in general has shifted drastically over the past decade.

Students now expect university presidents to take a firm stance on events taking shape outside of campus and around the world. Corporate CEOs, especially those of well-known public companies, are often expected by employees and customers alike to take a position on public policy matters such as immigration and climate change. We never used to expect this level of transparency or public responsiveness from leaders about their positions on social or world affairs. Obviously, there are a lot of challenges involved—a busy CEO must find time to develop a thoughtful approach to complex issues—but it can also be viewed as promising that we are gravitating toward a whole-person approach to running institutions. We're beginning to eliminate arbitrary barriers between work life and other matters. If customers are going to associate with an organization, university, company, or institution in civil society, they want to know what the leadership stands for. Every leader has to figure out how to navigate this world.

In YPO, we discuss local and global affairs and how they affect our lives, families, companies, and values. We have considered whether it would be advisable for someone to issue a statement or when a company should explicitly reveal its position on an issue. We've also discussed how to achieve agreeable disagreements in and outside of our companies and how to maintain civility and decency with respect to heated topics. I have enormous respect for the views of my YPO mates; listening to their challenges and approaches has been beyond valuable. I'm interested in the notion of enlightened leadership, particularly at a time of intense polarization and seismic shifts to the future of work, and I rely on the discourse and inspiration of fellow YPO members to chart a path.

A Real Impact

It's not often that you can interact with perfect strangers and form bonds almost immediately. But this is what happens with YPO. I've shared things with my fellow YPO members that I couldn't imagine sharing with other people.

Joining a YPO forum feels like being a freshman in college, when you walk into a dorm and connect deeply with people who seem like they were carefully selected to be your lifelong friends. The only other time I have experienced this is with my Aspen Institute Henry Crown Fellowship, where the group dynamic has a similar ethos. What I appreciate most about YPO is the solid friendships I've formed with people who understand the broader context of my life and in whom I have absolute trust.

YPO intentionally breeds such connections. The culture was built to attract and develop transparency and vulnerability. The fundamentals of the forum reinforce these ideals, which indicates how powerful the culture of any organization is.

Those who bring openness and compassion thrive and benefit the most from YPO's culture. In this sense, YPO is a self-fulfilling prophecy; you get from it what you bring to it. At least that has been my experience. It's my sincere hope that YPO members near and far have had a similarly meaningful experience.

PART TWO

NURTURING YOUR WHOLE SELF

CHAPTER SEVEN

A Family Tradition

Shannon Staglin, President of Staglin Family Vineyard

Shannon is president of Staglin Family Vineyard. After graduating from UCLA with a degree in cultural anthropology in 2001, she moved back to Napa to work as a harvest intern, learning about production and viticultural practices. In 2002, she honed her skills in marketing, hospitality, and consumer and trade sales.

After earning her MBA from the UC Davis Graduate School of Management, she worked outside of the wine business for several years. She was recruited to create the marketing program for Wells Fargo Family Wealth, providing multifamily office solutions for high-net-worth clients.

In 2011, Shannon returned to Staglin Family Vineyard, where she oversees all aspects of the business.

MY DAD WAS A MEMBER OF YPO NORCAL WHEN I WAS A little girl, and I have fond memories of attending weekend events organized for families. These events were mostly held in California at nearby locations, such as Lake Tahoe, but we once attended an event at a ranch in Utah, which had horseback riding for kids.

Since I grew up around the organization, I saw its benefits early on, especially in the interaction of kids my age. I was exposed to the educational opportunities the professional group provided in addition to fun, organized group activities, such as skiing. Even as a child, YPO offered unique experiences, such as when Scot Schmidt, the extreme skier, came to speak one time.

The Family Business

It has been my parents' lifelong dream to grow grapes and make wine in Napa Valley. Their dream became a reality in 1985, when they bought the property and released their first vintage a year later. In creating their business, they made sure to lay the foundation for its future by gifting a small portion of the estate to my brother and me.

Most kids—especially teenagers—don't want to take part in what their parents do, and I was no different. However, going away to college helped me gain perspective on my family's business and the unique opportunity it would provide me. After I graduated from UCLA in 2001, I moved back home to help out with the vineyard. I worked there until 2006, when I left to pursue an MBA. I then worked in banking from 2008 until the end of 2010 before returning to the family business, working my way up to my current role as president.

Unlike a lot of family businesses, my family is quite small, and we have a strong family foundation. As a result, we don't experience the typical struggles you hear about with other family businesses. Over the years, my parents have transitioned more and more ownership to my brother and me. We live by our mission statement, which is to create the highest quality wine possible, respect and serve our customers, conduct our business ethically, improve the environment, and have fun. YPO taught us the importance of a clear, shared vision.

My Role as President

The wine business is vertically integrated. As president, I oversee the day-to-day operations and touch all parts of the business, from the ownership of the property to growing the product to producing and selling our wine.

I work closely with our winemaker, Fredrik Johansson, on many decisions, such as blends and picking during harvest. I also work closely with our vineyard manager. We think about the day-to-day farming of the estate and the future of the property.

Not only do I oversee production and farming, but I also participate in client interaction sales. We sell 75 percent of what we produce to our mailing list and wine club members, but the other 25 percent goes to distributors in each state who sell our wine to restaurants and high-end retail accounts.

I travel a lot to establish relationships with sommeliers at some of the top restaurants and retailers around the country. I also travel and pour wine at events such as the *Wine Spectator* New York Wine Experience, which is an invitation-only event for international producers. The event includes top producers from France, the United States, Argentina, and Italy, among many other countries.

My Turn

Both of my parents were in YPO, so the organization has always been relevant to me both professionally and personally. When I officially joined, several good friends recommended the Golden Gate chapter. I was attracted to this chapter for several reasons, but primarily because I noticed a high percentage of female members compared to other chapters. I was also attracted to the focus on technology startups, because they're much different from the evergreen business I run. I admire and enjoy those who have an entrepreneurial and creative spirit.

When I joined YPO, I had a lot of different things to balance. (Don't we all?) I was engaged to be married, and I was busy planning my wedding while running the business. I was also hiring new team members to take over some of my responsibilities in national sales. I wanted to travel less and spend more time on the property so my husband and I could start a family.

Many challenges come with starting a family and raising children, not to mention the stress it places on a marriage. While I'm not sure balance is something that can ever be figured out, being a member of YPO made me feel like I'm not alone in my struggles.

Everybody in my chapter is at a different point in their life, and I find listening to their stories beneficial and inspiring. At YPO, nobody will ever tell you what to do or what not to do. Instead, they share their experiences openly and honestly and offer insight for you to make your own decisions.

Now that I am a parent, I realize my childhood experience with YPO taught me the importance of community. Children benefit when they're surrounded by intelligent people who are successful in their careers. In addition to the more common experiences school and sports provide for children, YPO provides another community for them to engage in and learn from.

Unlike Any Other Space

The forum experience at YPO is special and has been extremely helpful to me. Not only can members share their deepest fears and concerns in a safe setting, but they also listen to those who have gone through similar experiences.

My forum provides a place for me to discuss the highs and lows of business and a venue to share personal joys and grievances. Some of the most groundbreaking, meaningful, and memorable conversations in my forum have involved helping one another through difficult personal times.

Benefits beyond Business

Unlike the businesses of many other YPO members in my chapter, my company wasn't started to build and sell. Instead, it was built to transition down multiple generations. We don't aim for massive growth over a five- or ten-year period. We aim for gradual and sustainable growth.

I still benefit from my relationship with YPO members who work at companies that are vastly different from mine, however. Being surrounded by the energetic and creative individuals in my chapter pushes me to be better. They inspire me to think outside the box, especially since my "business box" is much different from theirs.

Moreover, the benefits of YPO extend far beyond business.

For example, we once organized a retreat to New Orleans. During our time there, we had the opportunity to work with Habitat for Humanity, an organization that builds houses for communities in need. New Orleans had been badly hit by Hurricane Katrina, and Habitat for Humanity was working in one of the flood zone areas. This retreat was particularly moving because we met with individuals who'd survived the flood and listened to their heart-wrenching stories. It was inspirational to hear how hard they'd worked to rebuild their communities. Although we were only able to help them in small ways, it was meaningful to connect on a personal level and give back in whatever way we could. It's an experience I will never forget.

When I think of my four and a half years at YPO, what jumps to the forefront of my mind is the long-lasting friendships I've made.

The relationships I create through YPO will last a lifetime. They are relationships that mean so much to me. The people in my forum have become like brothers and sisters. Whenever I need them, they will be there. It feels amazing to know that I can share anything, especially things that involve a lot of raw emotion. I trust them with my deepest feelings. There aren't a lot of places where people can express themselves that openly and honestly with no judgment whatsoever.

YPO is a one-of-a-kind organization, and it plays an important role in my life.

CHAPTER EIGHT

Looking at the Big Picture

John Welch, Founder of Making Fun, Inc.

John is a veteran product designer and leader of internet and mobile businesses. He is founder and CEO of Making Fun, Inc., a game developer and publisher creating mobile and PC games for digital platforms. Making Fun's titles—which include Eternium, Rune Strike, Ironbound, and Hidden Express—are created and operated by a combination of US- and Argentina-based employees and partnerships with talented external studios in Uruguay and Romania. He is a board member of game developer HitPoint Studios and a regular advisor to and faculty member of the annual Game Developers Conference.

WHEN I JOINED YPO, I WAS RUNNING A RAPIDLY GROWING company called PlayFirst. I started the company with a Power-Point deck and a lot of passion and industry experience but not much experience running a company. My co-founder quit his previous job once we had raised $5 million in venture funding. There we were with a big pile of cash and an empty road ahead of us.

Over the next few years, we did a lot of things right, growing to $1 million per month in revenue and over 200 employees and outside contractors. However, there were also many challenges, and I learned a lot about leadership—the hard way. It became clear to me that I needed mentorship to continue my growth and to remain effective as the company grew. I hired a coach and started looking at CEO peer organizations.

I was running something complex and unlike anything I had ever done before. The members of my board were constantly pushing me, often in different directions, and board management was my weakest skill at the time, followed closely by financial management. I was frugal with cash and a visionary within my industry, and I had deep skills in product, marketing, and engineering. I also had assembled an incredibly talented and motivated executive team and staff. However, I lacked the confidence and experience I needed to manage a venture board.

This ultimately led to my departure, and unfortunately, the company was sold for pennies on the dollar a few years later. Looking back, joining YPO a year earlier could have led to a drastically different outcome for that company and me. However, this is a story about the journey forward, not about what could have been. My experience at PlayFirst led me to YPO, and YPO has been instrumental in helping me develop as a leader, father, and friend over the subsequent decade.

A Look inside YPO

I was introduced to YPO by the founding partner of one of my venture investors during my search for peer leadership organizations. YPO stood out as the most prestigious group. It was criticized by people from other groups for not being purely business focused, but it was YPO's mix of business, personal development, and social activity that attracted me. YPO believes we are far more than our "business selves" and that exploring deeper and more broadly leads to profound growth.

I attended my first YPO event before I was an official member. My wife and I were guests at an end-of-year party at a member's home, which was a big, beautiful estate. Although the venue was imposing and the attendees were very accomplished, we immediately felt welcome. There was a sense of warmth at the party. These people were truly friends with one another. YPO wasn't merely a group of casual acquaintances or people looking for transactional returns. They enjoyed and cared for one another. As my wife and I met CEO after CEO and their husbands and wives, we were repeatedly struck by how genuine and down to earth they were. These people weren't exclusive or snobby. If anything, I noticed more humility in the organization than I had seen anywhere before.

That humility isn't accidental; it is a crucial part of YPO. The organization teaches you that for as much as you've accomplished and learned, there is always more learning and accomplishing to do. The more you learn, the more you discover you need to continue learning. I left the party honored to be included and excited to continue the YPO application process.

There are five YPO chapters in the Bay Area, and I joined the Golden Gate chapter, which is made up of about seventy-five members. While it is larger than many of the Bay Area chapters, it is much smaller than other big-city chapters. In cities like Boston, New York, and Los Angeles, for example, there can be more than 200 members per chapter. I appreciate that while my group engages with the other chapters in the area and across the international organization, we remain a tight, cohesive, and intimate chapter.

Every member in our chapter is also in a forum—which has eight to twelve people and is where the bonds of trust and friendship often become extremely strong. An ongoing theme for our chapter over the past several years is "Forum of 75." The theme reminds our members that even when in conversation with someone from outside our own forum, we should emulate a forum experience and aspire to go deeper and be authentic. I see our members practicing this approach all the time. One of the greatest things about YPO is that even if someone is in a different forum or chapter, we share the same backbone of experience, expectation of trust, and honest communication.

The YPO framework works. While we have social events and events focused on learning from experts, there is also a structured framework and process for the updates, explorations, and learning we do.

Before joining YPO, I didn't have a group of trusted peers interested in this type of growth. I wasn't surrounded by leaders who faced the same challenges I did. I didn't have relationships in which we could provide mutual value to one another through authentic feedback, listening, and sharing. I have now been a member of YPO for a decade, so I have a pretty good perspective on the before and after of the experience.

YPO's Pillars of Belief

It is easy to throw around concepts like honesty, confidentiality, and no judgment. However, these are genuine pillars of belief in YPO. In a forum meeting, everyone must feel like they can show up as their whole self. However, opening up is not easy. Not everyone can flip a switch and share their darkest secrets right away, and this was especially true for me. As excited as I was for YPO, I was far from "forum ready" when I started. One of the key strengths of YPO is how the institution of processes and people is set up to encourage members to grow and address their core challenges. More experienced people helped me get started on my journey, and a decade later, I have helped many people in turn.

An example of a core challenge might be sharing things that are deep, personal concerns with people in your forum, perhaps things that haven't even been shared with your spouse. Similarly, in sensitive business matters, informed but objective perspectives can be incredibly valuable.

A Look in the Mirror

A lot of people go through their lives without really looking in the mirror. At YPO, we are constantly looking. Because of my time in YPO, I have become a better father, husband, friend, and leader. I am more aware in all aspects of my life than I was before YPO.

Every member of YPO should be there to learn and improve. While we are able to join because we have achieved the required level of success, we are continually encouraged to look forward toward growth and improvement. Everyone is working on or toward something. The few people who leave YPO tend not to be ones who lack significant growth opportunities, but rather those who do not wish to face their challenges.

At a run-of-the-mill cocktail party, people often engage in

superficial conversations. At a YPO cocktail party, people often cut through the small talk and quickly reach a level of depth that gets to what is most significant. You can meet someone and only know them for a few minutes but operate as if there were a deep relationship because of the mutual framework of sharing, confidentiality, and trust.

Here is a great example. A few years ago, we had a chapter event at Alcatraz. On the boat from San Francisco to the island, I found myself in a conversation with another CEO in the chapter who wasn't in my forum. We started discussing an intellectual property issue he was facing in his company. I was amazed at the level of detail he was sharing with me. I asked probing questions, as I found the conversation to be intellectually fascinating. In any other scenario, I wouldn't likely have such an open and detailed conversation with someone I was just getting to know, especially a CEO of a public company. The conversation allowed him to blow off some steam and to get some practical value by presenting both sides of the argument and working through his thoughts with feedback from me.

On that boat, we were essentially in forum. He knew it was a safe zone and that I wouldn't repeat a word of the conversation to anyone. That impromptu "forum" experience is very memorable to me, partially because of the subject matter but more so because someone trusted me without really knowing me.

Deeper Interactions

YPO has taught me a lot about navigating life. I have learned a great deal from people who are different from me. In the past, I didn't put much thought into how people received my behaviors. Now, although I don't necessarily *change* my behavior, I think more about how I am being *received*. I'm not perfect, but

I am more purposeful and more nuanced now. Self-reflection—especially when it is assisted by those you trust—can be a powerful device.

I often implement and incorporate lessons learned through YPO at home. One of the biggest lessons I have learned, and subsequently tried to teach my children, is the power of being humble and admitting mistakes. Every person should acknowledge *their* role in any issue at hand. Can you imagine how much better the world would be if everyone shared this belief?

In YPO, we have a model of conflict resolution that involves sharing information without necessarily apologizing or defining right and wrong. A problem can often be alleviated through simple, frank discussion. Not all problems need to be solved. In many cases, mutual understanding can help clear things up. Conflict resolution is not always about solving a problem; sometimes, it is about putting our individual facts and feelings on the table and labeling them as such.

I teach my kids to consider how they are being received by other people. Is that how they intend to speak to people? Are they being too pushy? Do they want to be looked at as a complainer? These questions are oversimplified, and such issues often show up in a more complicated fashion for adults. However, my point stands: lessons learned in YPO are useful not only for the members but also for their kids—who have a lifetime to benefit from what they learn!

We all benefit from a better understanding of how we impact others. We should all take responsibility for our actions. We should all open ourselves up to learning. If you cannot acknowledge something, you cannot learn from it.

My mother died in 2002, and my father died just a few hours after my son was born in 2007. I was with my father shortly before his death, and though I wasn't sure if he could hear me, I said goodbye to him and told him I was doing what he would have done, which was flying across the country to be with my wife when our first child was born.

That moment still haunts me. When my son was young, I would often feel a foreboding sense of my own mortality. I stood over his crib and could almost feel my own death and a fear that I wouldn't be there to see him grow up. I was an only child and was very close with my parents; their early deaths gave me this foreboding feeling, like I had cancer and just didn't realize it yet.

Thankfully, I don't feel like that anymore, but it took a lot of time to shake that feeling. In a way, time heals all wounds, at least a little, but I tried to work through those thoughts with my forum. In addition to my wonderful wife, whom I am very close to, my forum and YPO chapter inherently offer a large and diverse support system. They keep me honest, help me up when I'm down, offer me ideas, and let me share my thoughts and work through issues.

Awareness and Accountability

I would say my job is atypical for YPO, but I also recognize that everyone's story is unique. A day after leaving PlayFirst in 2009, I bought a MacBook Pro and started writing iPhone apps to educate myself, because it seemed like an important thing at the time. This soon led me to start Making Fun with a few partners. We bootstrapped the company on revenue from clients, creating some of the first iPhone apps for the likes of *Vogue* magazine, Six Flags amusement parks, and the NFL.

We were about to start the process to raise funding for our own apps when we had the opportunity to sell to News Corporation and scale as a social and mobile game publisher from the inside. My YPO experience was invaluable throughout the process of selling, navigating the next two years leading a small company inside a massive corporation, and getting an unexpected opportunity to buy the company back when News Corp. changed directions and started selling off its smaller assets.

Making Fun has been independent since 2013, and I now work from home most of the time. We don't have an office in the United States, so usually, my commute is two flights of stairs. Other times, it involves two flights to another continent to visit our folks in Europe or South America. No matter how the specifics of my scenario might differ from those of my chapter members, I always find their advice and insight extremely valuable.

YPO has played a fundamental role in every transition my career has gone through. Over the years, I have discussed board matters, being fired, partner dynamics, selling the company, rebuying the company, fund-raising, and making difficult decisions to help the company survive. I have also supported others who have experienced major struggles with their boards and who have had to make difficult decisions to help their companies thrive. I have heard from countless other members regarding how they use YPO experience and support to navigate situations at work and at home successfully.

YPO has encouraged me to think carefully about what I want out of life and to make decisions from that place. I have learned to consider those things that give me strength, excite me, and make me want to get up in the morning. At YPO, no one makes your decisions for you. Nobody tells you what to do. YPO provides a safe place to think out loud and to hear shared experiences that might be relevant to your situation. The organization encourages but does not require members to be held accountable for making progress.

Personally, one big area of focus for me has been my goal to lose weight and get in better shape. Some members have heard me talk about this for almost ten years, but for a long time, I didn't make any real progress. In YPO, I explored the importance of being there for my children. I didn't want to be out of shape and risk dying young.

YPO gave me the element of accountability I needed. Admittedly, this included a little embarrassment about having had the same issue for so long. I knew it was something I needed to finally get to work on and do something about. Forums typically don't meet over the summer, which is when I finally managed to get serious about my health and fitness journey. I lost twenty pounds in a few months. When I next attended a forum, people barely recognized me. I attribute my success in this area to lifestyle changes enabled by support from my wife and the concern and self-reflection offered by my YPO forum. Who knows—maybe YPO helped to save my life.

Leaving Things Better than We Found Them

I am chair of YPO Golden Gate because I care deeply about the organization. I take the concept of being a servant leader seriously, and I am willing to do the work to hopefully leave the group a little stronger than I found it.

I've generally been an advocate for slow and constant progress. Revolutionary progress can be dangerous unless it is really necessary. Since becoming a chair, I've consistently reminded people that there are no right or wrong answers. Few matters are black and white. Instead, we must collectively think about the people in the group, what we want to be, and how aggressively we want to work to get there.

When I joined YPO, the chapter was around 15 percent female. At the time, that figure seemed normal to me. It was roughly representative of the percentage of female CEOs in the valley, maybe a bit on the high side. My forum had seven members in total, two of whom were women. Today, three of the eight members of my forum are women, which is a very high percentage given the market of qualifying CEOs.

YPO Golden Gate has historically struggled to recruit women. Going way back, perhaps there was little desire and then perhaps not enough focus. But those reasons are no longer true. The pool of available women who qualify for YPO is small to begin with, and the time commitment of the organization competes for time with families. However, those of us who have made this commitment have learned that allocating the time pays back disproportionately in personal growth that benefits our professional and personal lives. Those of us who volunteer as leaders in the organization get that extra multiplier where we get back even more than we give.

When I joined YPO, some forums didn't have any female members. There were just not enough women to go around. In some cases, people felt uncomfortable about mixed-gender forums. As a result, some women feel conflicted because they don't want to be a part of a group that has subgroups that exclude them. One of our goals in writing this book is to be open about the issues surrounding gender inclusion, including how to attract more women to YPO and how to educate both men and women about the benefits of mixed-gender forums.

Throughout my time at YPO, I've received feedback from men and women about their amazing experiences in mixed-gender forums. Still, inclusion inevitably brings certain challenges. When my forum gathers, nothing is off the table. For this to happen, it is important that everyone feels they can show up and share 100 percent of themselves. Everyone should feel comfortable being truthful, saying what's on their mind, and explaining how they feel.

For some people, however, religion might affect how open and vulnerable they can be. When we were embracing the issue of gender diversity as a chapter, few people thought about the impact of religion. A person might have religious beliefs that prevent them from engaging in certain types of conversations or sharing scenarios with members of the opposite sex. In attempting to respect rights and freedoms of gender, we find ourselves butting up against rights and freedoms of religion. Wow!

Not only is it important to address whether *men* want women as part of their groups, but it is also important to ensure that *women* are prepared to show up to these groups without judging those who might be different from them. Everyone should have an equal opportunity; however, that does not mean that we are all the same physically, emotionally, or in life experience. Some women might have never heard a man talk about some of the things men talk about in YPO. This is not surprising; society has traditionally trained us to show up differently based on the composition of a group. A conversation about gender inclusion cannot be simply how to get men to accept women; people must expect to encounter differences and to find common ground.

Fortunately, YPO arms us with norms and even formal processes that make this not only possible but also rewarding.

We Don't Have All the Answers

When I first joined YPO, my wife was part of an all-female partner forum, simply because there weren't many male partners opting to join partner forums. She later stepped out of the group because we had two little kids. Now that the kids are older, she is considering joining again. However, her initial impression when she heard about all of our forums being mixed-gender is that she doesn't feel as comfortable in a forum that includes men. She *liked* that her previous forum was made up entirely of women. Hmm. So, again, it is not as simple as getting men to accept and welcome women. Should there be places where men and women can gather separately? When thinking about YPO as a business network, one would immediately say, "NO!"—but YPO goes well beyond business, especially given how we welcome partners as just about full members of the group.

When it comes to inclusivity, we don't have all the answers. Obviously, we think it is important to make everyone who meets the qualifications of our chapter feel included. We want everyone to share the same beliefs about personal growth, sharing, honesty, and confidentiality.

One of the reasons that my forum has been so successful is because we don't think of ourselves as male and female. Instead, we are a group of people who have come together and embraced the ideals YPO stands for. Together, we have created a safe and comfortable environment.

In my opinion, the people who are most successful in YPO talk about these topics and face these issues head-on. That is how we learn and grow. YPO teaches people to be good, inclusive leaders, regardless of gender. As chapter chair, I am pushing my bounds of experience as a leader. Every member of YPO is strong, capable, and passionate. Every day, I make it my goal to help people with different opinions come to a consensus and make decisions that move the organization forward. I consider this a huge honor and privilege.

Sharpen Your Tools

The most common stopping point for people on the fence about joining YPO is time. Everyone thinks they are too busy to make time for yet another commitment. The way I see it, you have to stop to sharpen your tools. If you're not sharpening your tools every once in a while, you will inevitably underperform. The average person who hasn't participated in YPO might not even realize that their tools are dull. They might not understand that they have to do maintenance on their mind and soul every once in a while if they want to grow in wisdom as they grow in years.

While time is a consideration, the bottom line is that YPO provides an opportunity most people cannot get anywhere else in life. Not only is every member of YPO a CEO some are also moms and dads. Some are single. Some are running big companies, and others run small companies. Every individual enters the group with different life experiences. We all receive benefits from that diversity. I find it fascinating to think about, and occasionally even debate, how we can achieve true equality of opportunity despite our differences.

YPO has taught me how to observe more and to sometimes take myself out of my own emotions. You can be emotional, and you can be analytical. Try being analytical about your emotions—before, during, and after—and think about how you will be received. I've learned to intellectually engage with situations ahead of time, anticipating my actions and reactions in order to better control and define my behavior. Where is this most useful? Parenting! Of course, it is also very useful in the workplace and in life.

CEOs often joke that we want to hire people who are smarter than us to work for our companies. I want to hire a better engineer than me to write code, a better marketer to move product, and someone who's better in finance to manage the books. The same is true within YPO: we are always looking to raise the bar with people who can bring amazing attributes to our group. I am super-excited about what we've created at YPO, including and especially at YPO Golden Gate. I hope these thoughts have you a bit more excited to see what YPO could mean to your journey.

CHAPTER NINE

A Family Affair

David Krane, CEO of GV

David serves as chief executive officer and managing partner of GV (formerly Google Ventures), investing in a wide range of technology companies and overseeing the firm's global activities. Over the past decade, he has led the firm's investments in more than twenty companies, including Uber, Nest, Blue Bottle Coffee, and HomeAway.com. He currently serves on the boards of StockX and MGM Studios.

Previously, David served as a member of the senior leadership team that grew Google from a small startup to a multibillion-dollar global enterprise. Over the years, his professional experience has spanned both startup and public companies, including Apple, Qualcomm, Four11 (now Yahoo! Mail), and two computer security software developers.

YEARS AGO, MY WIFE AND I ATTENDED THE FIFTIETH birthday of a good friend of ours—MC Hammer. The event took place at a hip, funky venue in San Francisco called the Tonga Room, located in the Fairmont Hotel. The party was large and festive, as you'd expect of a guest of honor who is renowned for festivity and happiness.

As we mingled with other guests, my wife and I ran into a good friend of ours, who introduced us to the gentleman standing next to him, named Stuart. My friend was shocked that Stuart and I didn't already know each another and adamant that we should. Naturally, Stuart and I followed his enthusiastic lead and spent some time chatting. It turned out that our mutual friend had a point. We instantly clicked, and I knew I'd want to continue talking with Stuart beyond that birthday party.

Stuart asked whether I'd be free to meet him and one of his business partners for breakfast one day later that week. I said yes, and within a couple of days, the three of us met for breakfast at a classic Silicon Valley outpost.

I wasn't sure what to expect. I liked Stuart and wanted to get to know him better, but I knew almost nothing about his partner, whose name was Jody. Unbeknownst to me, Stuart and Jody had two reasons for wanting to meet me. One was simply to enjoy breakfast with a new friend. The other was to introduce me to YPO.

Although this was the first time I had ever heard of YPO, Stuart and Jody gave me a compelling overview. They described the powerful impact YPO had on their lives, including their business and friendship.

Both men impressed me, and I was intrigued by the taste of YPO they had given me. Jody had already "graduated" from his chapter and was affiliated with YPO Gold (the graduate organization of YPO), but Stuart was still actively involved in the Golden Gate chapter.

Stuart and Jody had a plan: get me interested enough in YPO that I pursued membership and then get me integrated into Stuart's forum. That's exactly what happened.

Following the meeting with Stuart and Jody, I went on to meet several other members of the same forum and learned more about YPO. My wife, Laura, and I attended a membership meeting and gave a presentation introducing ourselves, our family, my business, and Laura's pursuits when she wasn't busy chasing three children around. Shortly after, we were officially invited to join YPO.

A Personal Board of Directors

I joined YPO about the time I was ascending rapidly on a new career path at Google, where I have worked for almost twenty years. For the first decade at Google, I helped the founders build and scale the company, working as the company's marketer, storyteller, communications executive, and policy executive.

When I started out, the company employed fewer than one hundred people. Ten years later, Google had grown to 36,000 employees. When I joined, Google was a private company. Soon enough, it became a public company with billions of dollars in revenue.

My second career involved setting up a venture capital fund on the back of Google's platform, cash, and brand. I had transitioned out of working as a company operator and marketer and was learning the requirements of successful investment. I was highly focused on professional development.

I was attracted to the opportunity to contribute to YPO and learn from a small group of people. My YPO forum became my personal board of directors.

Some people in my forum are younger than I am, while others are up to ten years older. I love collaborating with this group on the most important areas of my life: my family, my business, and myself. Each of these pillars is addressed monthly—or more frequently—by the forum. We are all developing ourselves meaningfully across those axes with the support of the other members of our forum.

The forum experience and the relationships that have come from it have been the most valuable aspects of YPO for me.

When I joined YPO, I was forty years old. I had family and friends around me and was busy with my business. I never expected to come out of YPO with a dozen new best friends. These relationships have been an extraordinary side effect of my forum experience. For many of us, adulthood isn't a time to create rich and meaningful friendships. It's unusual for adults to make two or three new best friends, let alone a dozen. I feel so grateful and appreciative of this group of people. They have become special characters in my life.

We try to allow these unique relationships to spill into all aspects of our lives. Nearly half of the people in my forum have made a commitment to purchase and frequently use vacation homes in the same community. We also have pockets of density in several school communities, which has been special and very fun.

My Entire Family Benefits from YPO

My wife and I had no idea what to expect from YPO. This, I later learned, was partly intentional and par for the course. Applicants are told they are welcome to bring their spouses, but they aren't told how to integrate their spouses or how to handle the presentation required of each potential member.

Although the presentation is a source of tension for many applicants, I enjoyed that initial meeting. My wife and I had fun putting the presentation together and deciding which parts of our narrative each of us would share. Our lives are built as an equal partnership, and we engineered our presentation to include both of our voices. We both answered the questions asked after the presentation. Ultimately, Laura didn't become as involved with YPO as I did, but it was important to us that we present ourselves to the membership committee as a package deal from the outset.

I vividly remember one of the members practically tackling my wife after the meeting and recruiting her for the partner forum. That told me YPO was interested in *both* of us. Laura didn't join the partner forum, but she's a consistent presence at chapter events, which we enjoy attending together.

YPO's welcome extends to children as well. The chapter organizes a family-focused event once per year. This could be anything from an inside experience at the San Francisco Zoo to overnight camping in California's wine country. Our family often attends this event.

YPO also provides opportunities for members' children to visit Silicon Valley companies run by other YPO members. Kids get a deeper look at entrepreneurship, executive leadership, product development, and all the other factors that make Silicon Valley run the way it does.

Every fall, YPO organizes an experience for teenagers called YLAB. My oldest has attended and loved it. This year, I'm hosting an event myself. I'll be bringing a group of children of YPO members to my office at Google. My goal is to tell them the story of Google and explain what we do. I want them to feel like they are part of the company for a few hours. With more than seventy members, our chapter represents a diverse and interesting group of companies. Many of us are in tech and finance, but several companies represent a complete contrast to most people's perceptions of Silicon Valley.

My son found one of his YPO visits last year to be particularly impactful. He spent some time at a company called Revolution Foods, whose mission is to source, produce, and deliver better school lunches. Revolution Foods' main constraint is budget, which is $1.50 per meal per child per day. Some of the biggest questions the company faces center on how they can source, package, and deliver organic food for $1.50. My son engaged fully with the problems the organization faces, and Revolution Foods became a major discussion topic at our family dinner table.

Revolution Foods has also participated in a YPO chapter event for adults, which my wife and I attended. Every adult could explore product design and make meals within the constraints of that $1.50 budget. With the help of a celebrity chef from the local community, we were challenged to produce twenty meals on the spot. Thankfully, the chef helped us through some of the thornier parts of the process. When the food was ready, it was tasted by a panel of judges—students from an Oakland high school.

Perhaps the best illustration of how much YPO is woven into the fabric of our lives is the night our family decided during a dinner table discussion that it was time to get a puppy. We all agreed on the type of dog we wanted, and my wife explained that this particular type of dog is extremely popular and that we'd all have to be patient while we looked for one. We weren't going to find this puppy overnight.

At this point, my seven-year-old daughter suddenly asked, "Dad, can YPO get us a puppy?"

I looked at her in disbelief and then burst out laughing. YPO is not where you go to get a puppy, but clearly my daughter understood that the organization played a role in creating opportunities for our family.

I'm lucky that the energy of my forum is particularly supportive and welcoming. We do our best to arrange events that include members' partners and spouses, such as an annual winter holiday dinner. YPO gets involved in schools, parenting, sports, and extracurricular activities.

YPO has helped me as an individual, but when I think in terms of bringing my family into the fold, a whole new world of opportunities opens up. In my opinion, thinking about YPO as a family organization is the route to a richer and more inclusive experience.

Seeing the World with YPO

YPO gives members the chance to travel as a family by organizing trips for members and spouses, along with father-son, mother-son, father-daughter, and mother-daughter trips. Recently, I took my first father-son trip with my nine-year-old boy. Space was limited, and the twenty-six available spots sold out in just a couple of hours.

My son and I traveled to a ranch outside of Santa Barbara in Solvang. The weekend was packed with a huge range of activities. Some were designed to encourage father-son bonding. Others were led by expert child psychologists who taught us how to be better parents.

My son and I met YPO members and their sons from Chicago, Nashville, Texas, California, and Las Vegas. The weekend exceeded all of my expectations. What made me happiest was seeing how excited my son was. At the ranch, we learned secret handshakes with some other friends we'd made over the weekend. Since the trip, my son and I have been doing the handshake, looking at the photos, and remembering the great experience we had together and with other members.

About a year ago, I was invited to join a second YPO chapter. While my primary alignment is with Golden Gate, I also joined a group called YPO Intercontinental (IC). YPO IC comprises several dozen families from all over the world. This group is built exclusively around traveling together.

YPO IC was appealing to me for many reasons. The members and spouses Laura and I met were wonderful, welcoming, and inviting, and we met some of the families that had been part of YPO IC for a decade or more. The children of these families spoke warmly and passionately about growing up with the experiences curated by fellow YPO IC members. They fondly recalled all the great trips they'd taken, as children, adolescents, and college students. The older kids told us that the trips were so special they came home post-college to be part of them.

The group offers members four to seven trips a year to destinations all over the world. These trips are quota-limited and fill up fast. At the end of the fifth year, each member is asked to give back to the chapter and host an event of their choice, anywhere in the world. Members also have the option to co-host, instead of organizing the entire trip themselves. The aim is to create a unique experience somewhere special in the world. This can take place over a weekend or a week. As soon as members host one event, they are in the group for life. After that, newer members turn the wheel while older ones enjoy.

The group alternates between family trips and couples' trips—no trips are solely for members. Next summer, we'll take our first excursion as a family, joining a trip to Sweden. We're already counting down.

The Right Candidates for YPO

YPO is warm and welcoming, but membership must be selective to sustain the high quality of the group and interactions. For this reason, the recruitment process is rigorous. Every member has distinguished credentials and accomplishments, both personal and professional, and the potential to continue to do great things in the world.

When I meet people related to YPO, we naturally greet one another with respect. Even without knowing anything else about them, I know that every member of YPO is high functioning and high performing. Members typically are extremely impressive, kind, and committed to the organization.

Some people commit primarily to their forum rather than at the chapter level. This alone makes them happy and fulfilled.

In my experience, however, taking involvement in YPO to the next level and making investments in chapter, cross-chapter, and cross-organization relationships unlocks even more potential for greatness.

Almost everyone I've met through YPO is friendly, transparent, and easy to get to know. In a stunningly compressed period of time, I've learned a lot from nearly everyone I've crossed paths with in the organization. YPO brings out the best in those who join.

People sometimes ask me how people are chosen to be part of YPO. Personally, there are a few questions I ask myself when recruiting candidates:

1. Does this person have a superpower?
2. Can this person contribute something to us?
3. Can this person learn something from us?
4. Is this person just window shopping for an organization with allure? Does this person merely pitch well? Or is this person in a position to commit time and longevity to have a valuable YPO experience?

Members of YPO have a lot in common, but one big thing we share is that we're oversubscribed. We're all profoundly busy and never feel that we have enough hours in a day. This helps us to recognize both the commitment and the value of YPO. In order to attend a YPO event, we may have to sacrifice family time or risk getting behind in business. But we do it anyway, because we understand how important YPO is in our lives.

CHAPTER TEN

A Board of Directors for Life

Mollie Westphal, Owner M.W Investments

Mollie is the owner of a real estate investment trust and a developer in California. The company focuses on urban infill and mixed-use developments, sustainability, and acquisition of core assets. Mollie has started an opportunity fund focusing on tax-sheltered zones to better improve the communities around us. The company motto is "Doing well by doing good." Mollie is involved in many charitable organizations. She serves on the Dean's Leadership Circle and the President's Advisory Board at the University of San Francisco, and she recently accepted a position on the United Nations Women Empowerment Board. She is the past president of Balco Properties, Ltd., LLC, a commercial real estate company and a subsidiary of Bay Alarm Company, a third-generation family business.

I WAS ABOUT THIRTY-FIVE YEARS OLD WHEN I WAS INTRO-duced to YPO by a friend of mine in another professional group, Vistage. He told me he thought I'd outgrown the group. My business had grown much larger, and I was working on more complex projects, including development. He felt that I needed to be part of a more intimate and confidential conversation with a smaller platform. He went on to sponsor me to join YPO, for which I will always be grateful. Although I was excited to join YPO, at the time, I didn't realize what an honor it was to be invited to join the Golden Gate chapter.

I applied and was accepted, but unfortunately, I wasn't able to join. I was married at the time, and my husband felt it would become another commitment that reduced my time with him and the kids. That was a chaotic time for me, and I wasn't ready to fight for my right to join the organization. I separated from my husband four years later and called the organization to beg for another chance. The leadership team was reluctant to admit me; the application process for YPO is neither short nor easy, and I had gone through the entire process before only to turn down the opportunity without much of an explanation.

When I went in for a second interview, I explained to the committee that I had been through a terrible separation and divorce. When I first sought to join YPO, I didn't have the support I needed to make the organization a part of my life. On top of that, my children were little.

I do not consider myself a weak woman. However, everyone has to pick and choose their battles. I stood in front of the YPO team and explained as honestly as I could that standing up for my right to join YPO wasn't a battle I could fight four years earlier. I emphasized my desire to be a part of and contribute to the group. Thankfully, they accepted me.

Invaluable Support for Every Aspect of Life

YPO has played an essential role in supporting me through both personal and professional challenges. I work in a family business that functions as a holding company. My role is to run the commercial real estate business, which is one of several companies we own. We operate in four states.

When I joined YPO, real estate was just starting to bounce back from the global recession. While it had been a hard time, my company had managed our debt well. We could see the light at the end of a long, dark tunnel. It got so bad at one point that I hung a poster in the office saying, "Be calm and carry on." We had good debt-to-equity ratios and, therefore, were always in compliance and worked with our tenants and banks. Thanks to this ratio, the business grew considerably because of our cash flow and reputation for being conservative. Real estate investment trusts and local landlords were selling their assets at much lower rates than they had been previously marketed, so we took a chance on the market and acquired assets that had dropped to a reasonable price. We tripled the size of our business.

My personal life, on the other hand, was a different story. I had three young children and was going through an awful, acrimonious divorce. Meanwhile, the company was still growing, and my divorce represented an unwanted distraction. My ex-husband and I took joint custody of our children. Naturally, I worked much longer and harder during the times when I didn't have my kids. Work was the best distraction.

I recently decided to leave the family business. The decision has not been quick or easy—in fact, it's taken me three years. My experience with the company has been wonderful at times but difficult at others, and my interests led me to bigger projects. I wanted to work on something I could be proud of and something that would offer a great place to live and work in the community.

My company, M.W Investments, is developing 380 apartments with mixed use in downtown Oakland, California. It has been a challenging project that is breaking ground in 2019.

YPO played a vital role in helping me make the strategic decision to leave and live my best life. I couldn't have made the decision without them. We discussed whether I should leave, and if so, how. We have discussed both the emotional and financial sides of the decision. When I reached the decision to sell my shares in the holding company, my YPO forum supported me as I worked out the details. They encouraged me to stay strong throughout the process.

Selling my shares has been like going through another divorce. In my family, most of our wealth is tied into our companies. As a result, selling my shares has been like untangling a pot of cooked spaghetti. It hasn't been easy. Not only is it an expensive process, but it's also an emotional one. With the support of my YPO forum, however, I have faith that things are going to be fine. Everyone's getting along well, and I am lucky to have an amazing transition team and an incredible board helping me through. When the process is complete, I know I'll be left with a good-sized business and capital that I can grow into a sizable portfolio. I have a plan in place for the future.

YPO forums offer a type of support that is all too rare in most of our lives. Instead of giving advice, every member of YPO shares their experiences. Over the years, I've spoken to numerous people who have sold their businesses and worked through difficult partnerships. At different inflection points in my own journey, these people have helped me understand where to push for what I want and where to let go. They've helped me understand not to dig in my heels on the small points and instead to stay open to other solutions.

In business, it's easy to become emotionally attached. More often than not, the things we get attached to aren't all that important. To accomplish the bigger goal of selling my shares and working through my business, I had to let go of some things. It was incredibly helpful to turn to a group of people who've been through similar experiences in the past.

Throughout my career, my business identity has always been associated with my family name. The people I've met through YPO have helped me develop the confidence I need to build a brand of my own and carry out huge real estate deals solo. This is a major professional transition, and it has made all the difference to have the encouragement of my forum. They have helped me remember my own abilities from my twenty years in business. When I didn't think I could do it, they helped me realize that I can. YPO has provided me with the best network I could ever ask for. I feel confident that I could call anybody in the wider group and either ask for help or offer it.

A Board of Directors for the Whole Person

YPO provides members with a board of directors with whom they can talk about all aspects of their lives, including but not limited to their businesses.

Life is made up of many parts. None of us live all aspects of our life at once. When one area of our life becomes imbalanced, it's wonderful to speak to a familiar board of directors. At YPO,

I know I can speak confidently and honestly about my concerns. If it sounds like I'm avoiding something in the discussion, my forum mates will call me out on it. If I'm working myself to the ground, they'll encourage me to take a break.

Many business settings offer the opportunity to liaise with a board of directors, but most directors probably don't care much about other aspects of their CEO's life. YPO, on the other hand, cares about *every* element of members' lives. There aren't many places where we can be open and honest about every part of our lives and receive such high-quality feedback and motivation.

YPO never fails to surprise me. It's filled with accomplished people. Some have MBAs from Harvard, Stanford, or Princeton. I regularly meet people who appear to be absolutely perfect in every way. They run big businesses, are happily married to wonderful partners, and have beautiful kids. Even then, though, they've allowed me to realize that everyone is a little insecure at their core. No matter how much we have achieved, we all go through times of self-doubt, wondering if we're good enough or have made the right decisions. We ask ourselves, "Is this it?"

I'm a firm believer in constantly educating ourselves, through travel, listening, trying something that scares us, and being vulnerable. YPO is such a positive movement. Every person I meet through YPO is warm, friendly, and genuinely invested in making the organization better for everybody. My mission in life and my new business motto is "Doing well by doing good."

A Really Lovely Community

In essence, YPO is a really great, close-knit community.

The educational aspect alone is mind-opening. I'm studying for a program at Harvard called OPM. There are twenty YPO members taking part in it, and I was gratified to see many other women in the group as well as members from across the globe. We had open, insightful discussions. I believe these types of conversations can change the world.

YPO members are often leaders in their communities. Through open and honest conversations with other members, people gain a global perspective and bring that back to where they live and work. Little shifts have the power to create big changes. Based on my strong belief in this, one of my roles with YPO is as an advocate for the organization's university programs around the world. I've been lucky enough to spend time in Singapore and Turkey, and this year, I'm going to Africa.

YPO has affected me in so many ways that I struggle to pinpoint the most powerful example. One of my favorite aspects is the depth of the forum experience. I feel that I have formed such strong connections with the people in my forum. No matter how busy I am, I never regret attending a forum. I learn something, help someone, or receive help from someone.

I also benefit from exceptionally valuable connections. I'm starting a new opportunity fund, and in exploring different zones around the country, I found a real estate developer who is part of a YPO forum in Pittsburgh. I emailed him to explain my project and ask whether he knew of any good brokers I could talk to. As it happened, the day I planned to visit Pittsburgh was the day of his forum. He invited me to show up toward the end of his forum so he could introduce me to YPO over dinner and give me a perspective of the marketplace and opportunities there.

Just when I thought he couldn't get any nicer, he offered to take me around and introduce me to all the brokers in town. Needless to say, I had twenty-four incredibly productive hours in Pittsburgh. In that short time, I learned more about that market than I could have in months of my own research.

It's unbelievable how many people I have access to around the world, thanks to YPO. I'm constantly surprised by how quick and easy it is to reach out to people and how gracious people really are. Doors are wide open.

Looking to the Future

I was twenty-seven when I had my first child and twenty-nine when my youngest was born. Becoming a mother to three kids within the space of three years is a crazy experience, but before too long, that will change. In three years, right as I am on the brink of turning fifty, all three of my children will be out of the house.

With this impending transition in mind, I'm starting to think about my future with YPO. Within a few years, I'll be living an entirely different life as an empty nester. I've sold my shares, and I have my business and a great team.

Although I plan to work less in the last twenty years of my working life than I have up to this point, I still intend to grow, learn, and build new things. I want to empower my dynamic team as much as possible. I'm excited about the transition and the next fifty years. Who knows what they will bring!

PART THREE

BUILDING RELATIONSHIPS

CHAPTER ELEVEN

What Lights You Up

Jennifer Dulski, Head of Facebook Groups

Jennifer leads Facebook Groups, a product used by more than 1.4 billion people to create and participate in communities on topics that range from parenting and health to passionate hobbies and mobilizing around disaster response. She is an accomplished leader and entrepreneur with experience in successful startups and big-brand internet companies. Before Facebook, Jennifer served as president of Change.org, a social enterprise company that empowers people everywhere to start and win campaigns for change. Under her leadership, Change.org grew from 18 million users to more than 180 million, and thousands of social change campaigns were successful around the world.

Jennifer was an early Yahoo! employee, rising in the ranks over her nine-year tenure to ultimately lead one of the company's six business units as group vice president and general manager of Local and Marketplaces. She left Yahoo! to become co-founder and CEO of The Dealmap, a location-based deals site that Google acquired in 2011, making Jennifer the first woman to sell a company to Google. She is also the author of the Wall Street Journal bestseller Purposeful.

BY THE TIME THE DEALMAP (AN APP THAT ALLOWS USERS to browse deals based on their physical location) exploded, my co-founder and I had already tried a lot of things that didn't work. The Dealmap grew from nothing to several million users in the first year. We'd gone from trying so many things that didn't work to doing something that worked so quickly that it was hard to wrap our heads around what was happening. That period of rapid growth was very exciting. Companies such as Mastercard and Microsoft were cold-calling because they wanted to work with us. At first, I thought they were prank calls.

I started working in technology at a young age, right out of business school, and was at Yahoo! during the dawn of the internet. I rose through the ranks at Yahoo! quickly, and by the time I left, I was running one of six business units. When I branched out on my own, I had already led multihundred-million-dollar businesses and multihundred-person teams inside a larger company. However, The Dealmap was the first time I created something new.

Technically, I wasn't a founder of The Dealmap. I was initially hired as the CEO when it was a different company, but we ended up scrapping that idea and starting again with something completely different. The CTO, who was technically the founder, decided to call me his cofounder since we started from scratch together.

Overall, The Dealmap was a great experience. I had to think

about how to build a product people would love and how to structure a business that worked. It was fun and challenging. Adding to the challenge was the economic climate at the time. I started working there at the beginning of the recession in 2008, when raising money for a startup was tough. I worked hard to keep my team motivated through multiple rounds of failure in a difficult economy. That made our success even more exciting. We had been working so tirelessly for so long that it was wonderful to see it all pay off and to know that we built something people valued.

Shortly after I joined YPO, The Dealmap received an acquisition offer from another company. I had to decide whether to take more funding or sell. At the time, we had a term sheet for more funding and a merger-and-acquisition offer. It was a complex situation to navigate, since our board and investors were not in agreement about what to do. It was immeasurably beneficial to have my YPO forum there to help me think through that decision as a first-time CEO.

Joining YPO was an intuitive decision. I thrive in a community—my current job is helping support people who build communities, and I genuinely believe in the power of community to provide connection and support.

I also love that YPO provides both personal and professional support. One skill I've learned from YPO is how to quickly clear an issue through relationship building. When you care about your relationship with another person, you can mitigate conflict with them more easily. "Issues clearing" is a technique I have come to use regularly at work and just one of many things I've learned at YPO that have been directly applicable to my job.

Your Secret Team

My first forum was a mix of people who had been in YPO for many years and were about to graduate and people who were new to YPO and still early in their careers. Our chapter had many people who were about to graduate, so we brought in many new members. This gave us a bigger forum with a wider perspective.

While I was in this forum, we sold The Dealmap to Google, which was the right decision for where the company was at the time. I worked for Google for about eighteen months during the transition, which disqualified me from YPO since I was no longer running a company. In Silicon Valley, there are a lot of mergers and acquisitions, so it is common for people to join YPO when they run companies and later sell to a larger company. You don't qualify for a YPO membership grace period unless you have been a member for a year, and I had been a member for only eleven months.

Elizabeth Hutt Pollard, one of our chapter officers, went to YPO International to ask for an exception for me, since I was only a month shy of qualifying for that grace period. YPOI initially refused and said I'd have to leave YPO. At that point, something unexpected happened—without my asking them to, my entire forum wrote letters to YPOI asking for an exception, telling them about the value I brought to the group. Ultimately, YPOI granted me a waiver, and I was allowed to remain a member. That is a testament to how forums come together and what they are willing to do for one another. We sometimes call it our "secret team," because it's this group of people who will be in your court, no matter what.

After my eighteen months at Google, I began receiving calls

about other CEO and president positions. I bounced these decisions off my forum, trying to decide what to do next. I ended up taking the role as president at Change.org, which is a social enterprise company. After working for Change.org for about four and a half years, I decided it was time to pursue something else. I have evaluated different job opportunities twice now with my YPO forum. One of the things I've appreciated the most is the way they've helped me identify what really lights me up. They often see different things in me than I see in myself.

To help me think through my options of what to do next, we did an exercise called At Your Best, where I was asked to think about five times in my life when I have been at my best. These times could be work-related or personal. I had to describe the situations, what I was doing, and why I was happy. My forum listened to my replies and reflected back to me what they heard and what kind of venture might make me happiest based on what I'd shared.

Many people in my forum have had lifetime jobs, either by taking over family businesses or by founding companies and staying there. You might expect those people to advise me to do the same. However, based on my descriptions, their response to me was, "Jen, you really seem like a project person. You like to take on something, get it to a certain phase, and move on to the next thing." I hadn't realized that about myself before, but it was true.

My first job out of college was as an entrepreneur founding a nonprofit. The program was built to help under-resourced children be the first in their families to attend college. After my first year, I hired a co-director, and three years later, I passed the program on to him to run. This year is the program's twenty-fifth anniversary. It is still thriving, having had many different directors over the years, and preparing thousands of first-generation college graduates. It's one of the things I am most proud of in my life.

The same thing happened with Change.org. My job was to get it to scale, building out the teams, processes, and business models it needed to be successful. After navigating several challenges, we got the company on the right track—it's growing faster than ever and will be profitable this year. When it was clear that the work I'd set out to do was done, I found someone to replace me and went on to do something else. My YPO forum mates helped me realize that's my superpower, which is different from many others in my group. That is one of the best things about YPO. It encourages people to share experiences that may have value for others but never assumes that experience applies to everyone else.

When I decided to leave Change.org, I was mainly looking at CEO positions for midsize companies. I found an opportunity that was attractive, but then I got a call from Facebook, which had recently changed its mission to focus on community. Facebook invited me to lead Facebook Groups—the center of community work on the platform and a product used by nearly 1.5 billion people. I had to carefully look at my options again and consider how important the CEO role I was seeking really was to me. I called an emergency meeting with my forum (you can occasionally call your secret team to an emergency meeting for those who can make it) and told them I was debating between these two positions. They said if creating impact in the world was at the top of my list, then there wasn't another job that could do it at the same scale as Facebook. That sealed the deal.

Communities Need Contributors

All communities need contributors, and YPO is no different. For as much as you gain by being a part of YPO, you also must contribute, and your first contribution is your physical and mental presence. Coming to events, being on time, listening to peers, not being distracted by your phone or computer—those are at the core of what makes YPO work. Between educational events and forum meetings, we meet about one day per month. Getting that many hours of uninterrupted time from people who can help you is a truly valuable resource. For that reason, I make sure to give my focus and attention to the other members in return.

At Facebook, we all sit at desks in an open area and executives get dedicated conference rooms, which have names. I call mine Hosting a Party, because we believe that great community leaders are like great party hosts. They invite people to join, make introductions, start and nurture conversations, and break down conflict. In communities, people are more willing to be vulnerable and share if someone else already has, so I try to model the level of vulnerability and openness that we want the whole community to have. When you hear and understand things that are going on in other people's lives, it makes you feel more comfortable talking about what's going on in your own.

That is something I see in the communities being formed on Facebook. Many of them are about topics such as parenting and health issues. These communities are full of people who are supporting one another by sharing their own experiences. This gives people the sense that they're not alone. While these groups are effective online, they're even more effective when people find ways to connect in person.

That is what I have with YPO. It's a community of people who may not be dealing with the same thing I am but who have experiences that allow them to offer advice and support.

When I joined YPO, my daughters were ten and eight. Now they're eighteen and sixteen. Seeing how other people approach parenting—from struggles in school to mental health issues and college applications—has been invaluable. Some people in my forum have adult children, some have babies, and some don't have children at all. Having a community with such a broad range of life experience is what makes it work so well.

YPO Is a Meaningful Community

I've been in three different forums over my eight years with the organization. YPO teaches you to build deep relationships with people fairly quickly, and we implement this at one-day "Stir Fry" forums, where we mix people from different forums together to better understand people throughout the chapter.

I am a big believer in the power of community. At Facebook, we've conducted research, including academic literature review, surveys, fieldwork, and data analysis, on what it means to be part of a community—and, in particular, what it means to be part of a *meaningful* community. We've defined "meaningful community" as a gathering of people in which individuals gain a sense of connection, belonging, and safety, and where you give trust and investment over time.

We have tested this in every country in the world and have come to the same definition each time. Based on this research, I can confidently say YPO is a meaningful community. I feel a deep sense of connection to these people. I feel safe in the environment we've created. I trust that I can share sensitive things, both professionally and personally. And I work hard to give back to the community to continue making it stronger, both for the people who are part of it today and for those who will join tomorrow.

CHAPTER TWELVE

From the Heart

Zhengyu Huang, Founder of Yu Capital

After working as a managing director at Intel and as a White House fellow in the Obama administration, Zhengyu founded a financial services technology company in Shanghai in 2009. His firm connects global institutional investors with opportunities in emerging markets. In less than ten years, it has grown to include eight offices employing 300 people across four countries.

Zhengyu has worked in more than ten countries and traveled to more than seventy. His experience has given him a rare perspective on the globalization of business and finance, and his company has helped investors raise and invest tens of billions of dollars. Zhengyu has spent half of his twenty-year career living in China and half in the United States. Recently, he decided to make his permanent home in the San Francisco Bay Area.

ABOUT THREE YEARS AGO, I REEXAMINED MY LIFE. ALthough I was born in Shanghai and knew the city to be vibrant and fast paced, I also found it to be transitory. People come for a few years and enjoy the hustle and bustle, then leave. I met a lot of interesting people and enjoyed the energy of Shanghai, but I was not building many deep, long-term relationships.

My father had passed away, and my mother was getting older and living in the United States. I wanted to spend more time with her. I was also feeling the urge to get married and start a family, and Shanghai did not feel like the best place to do that. Since I no longer had an operational role with my company, I decided to move back to the United States.

Although I enjoy many US cities, I chose to live in San Francisco. I had gone to school at Stanford, just south of the city, and I still had many good friends in the area. It's the people who make a city great, and I knew I would be comfortable in the Bay Area. Still, I'd been away for several years and would have to make new connections and build fresh networks and communities. That's when I thought about YPO. I had learned about it several years prior, but the timing wasn't right for me to join then. Now it felt like it was. I was wrestling with some big private questions: How could I develop a better relationship with my mom? How could I prepare myself for married life and everything that it entailed? I needed a group of trusted people to talk to and share with.

How YPO Fit into My New Life

I made the move and quickly became busy in San Francisco, where I picked up two new businesses. One company was a derivative of my previous venture in Shanghai, and the other was a journalism startup. Juggling two companies was hectic, but I enjoyed the challenge and learned a great deal.

Despite how busy I was, I made time for YPO. I went for an interview and was impressed with how open, honest, and direct the interviewer was. He told me what he liked about YPO and what he didn't like. He also shared what I could gain from YPO and what I should consider contributing.

I went to my first forum with a little trepidation. There were seven other people in the group, and they had been together for more than five years. How was I going to fit in? I assumed it would take some time for me to be accepted, but right from the start, the other group members shared information about themselves and listened closely when I spoke. Clearly, these people trusted one another and valued my views, which made me feel welcome. By the end of the session, I felt like each person was an old friend.

My time at YPO has taught me a tremendous amount about leadership and empathy. I've learned to lead from the heart rather than from pure logic. I'm more aware of my emotions and the emotions of those around me. I ask myself positional questions now such as, "Where is this person right now?" rather than, "Is my logic getting through to this person?" These are skills that I need to continue working on, but YPO has taught me how to reflect and improve. It's not easy to change a lifetime of habits, but my forum has supported me and helped me learn how.

While we discuss business at YPO, our discussions are often more profound than the nuts and bolts of leadership and decision making. How can I quickly improve my leadership skills? How can I radically alter my engagement framework with other people? This isn't necessarily business, but answering these questions makes you a better person, and that's good for business.

My forum also gives me the personal support I need as a CEO. Being a CEO is stressful work, but at YPO, we bolster one another because we often face the same challenges and pressures. I am always thinking about what I want to get out of the forum and what I want to contribute to it. We all want to improve. We are all high-achieving CEOs and desire the best from everything we do, so pulling the most value for ourselves during those four hours is a shared, common objective.

Last year, I became a moderator for my YPO forum. I felt like there were things that could be improved on, and instead of just sharing my ideas, I wanted to step up and challenge people more. As a moderator, it's up to me to make sure we discuss topics that are helpful and meaningful to everyone. I look for ways to foster the bond among forum members. It's easy—and even helpful—for people to come in, talk for four hours, and then leave. But when we build deeper personal connections, the discussions and relationships are more rewarding. These relationships often spill into other aspects of our lives. I've exercised with other members, grabbed dinners, and socialized with them. Some of my best friends for life are from my forum, and I think that's what every forum aspires to.

Each forum has its own personality; some are relaxed, while others are more focused and serious. Some groups hang out all the time outside of the forum, while others remain focused on business. Members determine the personality of their group, and the initial interview process helps forums find like-minded new members.

I dated a woman for about a year, and we often talked about my relationship in the forum. Everyone in my YPO group met her, and members have been generous with their support and advice. They truly cared for her. Everyone in my forum is married except for me, so I benefit from their experience and insight. That has been more valuable than I could have imagined.

Once a year, our forum breaks away for a weekend retreat where we can focus on making substantial breakthroughs. I've been to two so far, and they are particularly rewarding. You come away from these retreats—and all of our gatherings, for that matter—with a high confidence in your ability to relate to anyone and everyone. You develop the ability and willingness to probe issues deeply and intimately, and great insight comes out of the practice.

You also develop sincere gratitude for having this group to share time, issues, and feelings with. Two years ago, I didn't even know these people, and while I might not be involved in their daily lives, I know deeply personal things about them. That's how life should be—authentic and at the most human level possible. We should not be afraid to feel vulnerable, to ask questions about how to face life's biggest challenges, or to accept that life's biggest problems are often internal rather than external.

The YPO forum is such an important part of my life that I have flown back from Asia just to attend a meeting. For the forum retreat last year, I flew in from Asia and then back to Asia when the weekend was over. This represented twenty-four hours of flying—twelve hours each way—but it was worth it.

Because YPO is a global organization and I travel frequently, I meet new friends everywhere. I was recently in Hong Kong for a YPO conference and will be in Montreal in a couple of weeks for another YPO conference. Still, meeting with my home chapter in the Bay Area—where my group's businesses, homes, and families are—helps me feel rooted and grounded. My personal story has both domestic and international chapters, but with YPO, I don't have to choose one over the other. I can live and reap the rewards from both sides of my life, and I'm grateful for how YPO has helped me achieve that balance.

CHAPTER THIRTEEN

Part of My Village

Kristin Richmond, CEO of Revolution Foods

Kristin is the chief executive officer of Revolution Foods, which she co-founded in 2006 to transform the way we feed our students in this country by serving healthy meals and offering nutrition education to underserved schools and city programs across the nation. Before founding Revolution Foods, she was vice president of Resources for Indispensable Schools and Educators, where she designed and executed a strategy that grew the organization from a small, community-based program to a nationally scalable model working with more than 700 teachers and 60 public schools. In 2007, she won the Global Social Venture Competition for the Revolution Foods model.

Kristin began her career in investment banking at Citigroup. She also lived in Nairobi for two years, where she co-founded the Kenya Community Centre for Learning (KCCL). She was a member of the White House Council for Community Solutions and is a board member of Lighthouse Community Public Schools and UC Berkeley's Global Social Venture Competition. In 2010, NewSchools Venture Fund named Kristin and her co-founder,

Kirsten Tobey, Entrepreneurs of the Year. Kristin is an Ashoka Fellow, an Aspen Institute Fellow, and a Young Global Leader at the World Economic Forum.

I CO-FOUNDED REVOLUTION FOODS WITH A VISION TO dramatically increase access to healthy, affordable, beautifully designed foods in our most at-risk communities across the country. We meet families where they are to provide healthy, chef-crafted meals that are made from clean-label ingredients—no artificial anything. This was a new model in the food world when we started. Today, we procure, design, manufacture, and distribute close to 3 million healthy meals per week across 3,000 school and community sites. We serve big, urban districts such as Boston Public Schools, San Francisco Unified, and Newark Public Schools; large charter school networks; and national networks such as the Boys & Girls Clubs and YMCA. We're in over 400 cities in 15 states, working with mayors, superintendents, and after-school program leaders to create healthier communities citywide.

Thirteen years in, we are on track to be a $170 million company in 2019. We have seen a lot of growth, and building Revolution Foods has been a labor of love. The thing we are most proud of is that we now have third-party research data connecting our approach to citywide wellness and nutrition with improved academic outcomes for our children. It is exciting to have data linking our meal products and broader work to the academic outcomes of our youth.

Adding YPO to My Village

I was working as a first-time CEO at a VC-funded company

when I was approached about joining YPO. The woman recruiting me was enthusiastic—she had vetted me with several
of my board members, who vouched strongly for me—and I met
her for lunch in San Francisco to tell her I was very interested.
I was also extraordinarily busy. I was working on a White House
council under the Obama administration, I was a new CEO
managing a pioneering approach to an antiquated industry, and
I was a brand-new mom of two small boys. On the one hand, I
wondered where I'd find time for YPO; on the other, I realized
I needed help juggling all of this.

We all need a supportive village around us, and a CEO can't
necessarily go to her board of directors or team for that kind
of support. Having a group of people available to help work
through tough issues seemed like a valuable resource. I knew
there would be more challenges to come and that others in YPO
would be right there with me.

I wanted to add YPO to my village because I was aware of the
complex dynamics I faced in my company and the challenges
that would come with trying to grow quickly. I wanted to go
from stage one to stage ten, but I didn't know precisely how to
do that. I knew I would need to grow significantly in my leadership abilities and appreciated that YPO was a place where leaders could connect confidentially and learn from one another.

YPO at Work

YPO has provided a safe space for me to manage difficult
situations at work, such as a key and beloved employee who
was incredibly sick and who unfortunately passed away after
struggling with cancer for many years. Having a place to talk
about that was invaluable. I could ask others how they handle

things like this in their companies. How do they support people when they're ill? How do they develop a realistic view of what that employee can and can't do? It is important to talk about these issues with neutral parties who don't work directly with the person in question, so as not to potentially impact their employment.

I have talked with my YPO forum about conflicts I've had on my team and questions about strategy when building my board and investor base. They've helped me with decisions around growing a company from zero to $170 million and close to 2,000 employees. They've also helped me with questions about profitability. As a company that serves healthy meals to big public schools and institutions, we have a tight margin. I wanted to drive efficiency and protect our mission and quality of products but wondered how best to do that. Two or three of my forum members suggested that I create a continuous improvement effort and advised me how to build it, whom to talk with, and how to design the system. I have learned so many company-building strategies from these people that I couldn't begin to list them all.

One highlight of my time with YPO was co-organizing our chapter retreat to the Supreme Court. Our chapter visited DC right in the midst of the Brett Kavanaugh hearing, a major moment in our Supreme Court's history. Having the opportunity to be there during this pivotal time in American politics was a once-in-a-lifetime experience. I expected to be most impressed by the legal process, the history of the court, the grandeur of the setting, and the complexity of today's political landscape, but I stepped away from that experience with something different. I came away with complete and utter respect for and fascination with the teamwork the eight justices demonstrate, despite coming from different perspectives. I was completely focused on the leadership, teamwork, dynamics, and culture that our justices have built and am encouraged to take what I've learned and use it to improve my own company's work culture.

YPO at Home

On a day-to-day basis, you have to gather support around you to keep yourself motivated and able to function successfully. My YPO forum is part of the village that makes my life run. That village also includes my husband, who is the most amazing partner in the world, and my co-founder and her amazing husband. Whether it's your husband, partner, grandma, mom, or anyone else, having community support is critical, especially when you face the pressures that come along with leadership and company building.

YPO understands this—the organization even offers a partner forum for working spouses of YPO members. My husband has been a member of that forum since day one. It's been helpful for him because he is also an entrepreneur, and it's often hard for others to understand what it's like to build a family with two people in our positions. The partner forum allows us to appreciate the experience of YPO together. We both reap the benefits of the program.

My kids are part of the community, too. While I don't want to sugarcoat the reality that moms and dads face trying to balance work and family, my children and my family are a true source of inspiration and strength. My boys are nine and twelve now, and I have always worked. Part of what keeps me going is when my kids say, "Mom, you could never leave Revolution Foods. You feed millions of kids, and they need you."

While your kids inspire you, you inspire them. My son recently asked if I could speak to his class about entrepreneurship, which makes me feel good about how my kids see me and my work. My kids also see women in business differently than many people. That really struck home a while ago when my son asked me why I had to travel to New York City early one morning and who I was meeting. I explained that I was meeting a CEO who could meet only at this specific time. He asked, "Why can't she meet you later?" He took it for granted that the CEO would be a woman.

I spend a lot of time talking to women who aspire to be leaders, and they are often concerned that they can't "do it all." It's true there will be trade-offs, but sometimes being a woman or a mother actually makes you more authentic in your job. At Revolution Foods, we are in a business that specifically serves youth, families, communities, and parents, but almost every business does, if you think about it. I feel that running this business while raising a family has helped me speak to our audience, consumer base, and decision makers in a way that is authentic when considering the challenges each of them faces day to day.

As we design products, we have kids and parents in mind, and it has been helpful to have my own kids as product testers. Kids in general are very tough critics—they'll tell you what they really think. Having my kids give me that kind of feedback has been grounding, because I know what I'm creating will resonate with other children.

Youth Learning About Business (YLAB)

Having the chance to host YLAB was a special experience for me. My only regret is that my children weren't old enough at the time to participate. I got to connect with middle- and high-school-aged kids and talk to them about entrepreneurship, having a vision, and creating something from square one. We talked about everything from designing with your consumer in mind (in our case, youth like them!) to how they could have a positive impact on the world through entrepreneurship.

Then we went into food and its design, because a big part of our promise at Revolution Foods is to create culturally relevant, chef-crafted, kid-inspired meals. We like to collect consumer-based insight, and who better to ask than the thirty kids in the room with me?

These were the kids of YPO leaders, not necessarily the group we serve, but the tone in the room was all about getting involved. The kids wanted to know what they could do right now. They were aware of their privileged background and ready to use those resources to give back. They wanted to make a difference. One of the most exciting things happening right now in our country is the growing voice of the youth. We should get excited about that and try to spark that empowerment early and actively.

While my kids aren't yet old enough for YLAB, they have enjoyed special YPO educational events. We went to the San Francisco Zoo, and they asked the zoologists caring for the lions about habitat, why zoos exist, and how they are promoting conservation. They had a million questions, not just in the lion area but also in different parts of the zoo: elephants, giraffes, and birds. They told me it was "the most amazing thing in the world."

Impact of YPO

I have stayed committed to YPO for many reasons—the quality of people in it, its impact on my growth as a leader, and the learning I have been able to bring back to my team, my board, our mission, and my family. I can't say enough about the benefits YPO has brought into my life.

When I was growing up, I was taught to work hard, put my best foot forward, and shoot for the stars. My mom always told me that I could do anything. Today, I'm on a mission to inspire kids, to plant a seed that creates a big impact. It all starts with one person, one idea. If you gather a group like YPO around creating that impact, it's amazing what you can do—you may well reach those stars.

CHAPTER FOURTEEN

Bonds That Last

Gabriela Parcella, Executive Managing
Director at Merlone Geier and Director
at Terreno Realty

*Gabriela is executive managing director at Merlone Geier Part-
ners and an independent director at Terreno Realty Corporation
(NYSE: TRNO). Before that, Gabriela was the chief executive
officer, president, and chair of Mellon Capital Management Corporation. At Mellon Capital, Gabriela was known as a collaborative, team-oriented leader who managed complex demands and
oversaw and coordinated the fully integrated $380 billion AUM
company. In addition, Gabriela chaired Mellon Capital's board of
directors and the executive planning committee and was a member
of the BNY Mellon senior management group.*

*Gabriela chairs the board of the Schools of the Sacred Heart San
Francisco, serves on the Stanford Law School Board of Visitors,
and is a member of the Stanford Real Estate Council. She was
ranked third on Fortune and ALPFA's "50 Most Powerful Latinas
in Corporate America" list in 2017.*

I WAS RAISED IN THE BORDER TOWN OF EL PASO, TEXAS,
after my parents immigrated to the United States from Mexico

in the sixties. They made that move to give their children more opportunities than would be possible in Mexico. Having a chance at the American dream was so important that my father risked his life by serving in the Vietnam War, even though he wasn't yet an American citizen.

I give a lot of credit for my success as a CEO to the way I was raised. My parents sacrificed a lot for us to be here. They always emphasized education, family, and integrity. I was encouraged to do my best in every endeavor and not to squander any opportunity that might present itself. Because of their efforts, I was able to go to the University of Texas at Austin for my bachelor's degree in business administration and my master's in professional accounting and then to Stanford Law School. Moving to California and attending Stanford Law School changed the trajectory of my career and my life. I was transformed by the people I met, the education I received, and the community that I became a part of on the West Coast.

A friend recommended YPO as soon as I became a CEO. I was forty-two at the time, and he emphasized the importance of applying quickly so that I would meet the under-forty-five age requirement. At first, I was concerned about the time commitment of YPO. I was stepping into a CEO role that required a lot of travel, I had two young sons, I was on the school board, and I had recently joined the board of Meals on Wheels. I wasn't sure I could take on one more thing, and I knew that YPO was a serious commitment.

I also wasn't sure what type of culture and environment I would find in YPO. Then I met Elizabeth Hutt Pollard, who was in charge of membership. She was down to earth and warm, and she assured me that I could manage the time commitment and get a lot out of YPO. I also went through the traditional process of meeting several members for lunch.

I was sold. The members were all welcoming and incredibly interesting.

What surprised me most was that almost all of the YPO members I met were self-made. These aren't people from wealthy families—most of them are people like me who worked hard and figured out a way to start or grow a business. That is part of what makes the group so welcoming to everyone; it's composed of individuals who decided to create something and made it happen. It was inspiring to meet all these creative and impressive people.

Learning from My YPO Colleagues

I was with Mellon Capital for twenty years. I started out as a junior lawyer in 1997, became the general counsel, and eventually moved to the business side, becoming chief operating officer (just in time for the 2008 financial crisis). Having done a good job of navigating through the financial crisis, I became the CEO in 2011.

With my COO experience and thirteen years under my belt at Mellon Capital, I felt very prepared to run the business. However, I felt less prepared for the external requirements, such as speaking engagements. I had attended a lot of investor meetings, so I understood that piece, but public speaking at conferences and events was something new. Fortunately, I was able to speak with other YPO members who had made the same sort of transition. They shared with me how they prepared, how they trained, and what resources they used to become better public speakers.

I was also able to talk with other YPO members about the challenges that come with being a Hispanic woman in business. First and foremost, being a first-generation American has given me an advantage—it has made me very motivated to succeed and never waste what I have been given. At the same time, I had big shoes to fill, as I was replacing a beloved CEO and was the first female CEO at Mellon Capital. Like Mexico, the financial services sector is very male dominated, and I think that background made me acutely aware of possible barriers I might have to overcome.

At first, I wasn't sure if the members of my YPO forum would understand what I was experiencing as a Mexican American woman running a large global investment management firm. I naively thought that you needed to be in my same industry to understand my challenges (and successes). What if they were all in technology, consumer packaged goods, or some other industry? Could we still learn from one another?

It turned out that, of course, we could and did learn a lot from one another. YPO isn't about your industry at all—it's about leadership, which is the same regardless of industry. In the end, several member CEOs, men and women, served as sounding boards for my career. They all had unique experiences to share, and I learned something from each and every one of them.

As it turns out, being a Mexican American CEO has not been the obstacle I feared it might be. In my role as CEO of Mellon Capital, I traveled to countries where they are not used to seeing many female CEOs, such as Japan and Chile, and even there, I felt very comfortable and was often told by our clients that they saw me as a role model for their efforts to advance women.

Making Big Moves

When it came time to leave Mellon Capital, YPO helped me with that, too. Making the move was hard, because I had been with Mellon Capital for twenty years. However, I had seen several other CEOs in YPO successfully transition from one company to another. Just knowing I wasn't the first to do it was immensely helpful.

I also got some practical help from one of my YPO colleagues, who introduced me to the CEO of a real estate company that was looking for an independent director. I ended up joining the Terreno Realty Corporation board and through the process met the co-founder of Merlone Geier Partners. I joined Merlone Geier Partners and am loving every minute of being a part of a private investment management firm. It is an entrepreneurial company and very collaborative. It's also a place where you can invest alongside our institutional investors, which creates great alignment. It's freeing to be part of a privately owned company after coming from a highly structured, bank-owned investment management firm. The transition from CEO to partner has been great. I love investing in real estate, the long-term investment horizon, and the lack of bureaucracy.

Changes in YPO

Over the years, as my professional life has changed, YPO Golden Gate has changed, too. Every forum now includes men and women. I was fortunate to always have at least one other woman in my forum, and that was very important to me. When we go on retreats out of town, it would have felt uncomfortable for me to be the only woman (perhaps because of my Hispanic upbringing). Fortunately, I never had that problem, and now, our forum has close to a fifty-fifty split of men and women.

When Elizabeth managed membership, YPO was specifically recruiting women. As a result, the Golden Gate chapter became known as a woman-friendly chapter, and that focus turned out to be a self-fulfilling prophecy: once we got a reputation for being welcoming to women, more women came.

Cultural diversity within YPO has gotten a lot better, too; however, it can always improve. As more people from different cultures, countries, and backgrounds join, it will draw more diversity into the organization. Socioeconomic diversity remains a challenge, partly because joining YPO requires that your company has to be a certain size, so those who qualify tend to have been in business awhile.

YPO will continue to evolve over time, as members who turn fifty leave and new members come in. The forums are continually being refreshed.

The Impact of YPO

This is my last year in YPO, because I just turned fifty. When I first joined YPO, I thought it would just be a business networking group. Everyone tells you it isn't, but it is hard to imagine anything else until you've experienced it. I was surprised to find that YPO is about meeting people who are going through the same things you are and supporting and being supported by them. It's different from a traditional business roundtable of pure networking. YPO is that place where everyone understands the issues you face as a CEO.

I feel it's important for women to invest in themselves by joining YPO. It is a big-time commitment, true, but if you think of it as an investment in your own development, it is very worthwhile.

Most women don't prioritize doing things for themselves. Between work, kids, and caring for other family members, we can feel very stretched. Once I thought of YPO as something I was doing for myself, I was able to become comfortable with the time commitment. We typically meet one full day per month between September and May. This may seem like a lot, but you end up feeling recharged and rejuvenated from the experience, which makes it worthwhile. I have never left a meeting feeling like I shouldn't have gone or wishing I had stayed at work. I always feel refreshed and full of new ideas.

As I think about leaving the Golden Gate chapter, I am most grateful for the friendships I've developed over the last seven years. Leaving is very bittersweet, and I will definitely miss Golden Gate, but I also feel like it's time to make room for the younger CEOs. That is the point of YPO: to be with people who are going through the same things you are and work through them together. As I head into a new stage in my life, I will look into joining YPO Gold (the chapter for members over fifty).

The beauty of YPO, for me, is that its value compounds over time. There isn't one event I can point to as the pivotal moment, but all of the small interactions combined have made it a wonderful experience. Having had a consistent group of people I could go to with any question, challenge, or success—and knowing that they would be there for me in a genuine way—has been priceless.

PART FOUR

DIVERSE PERSPECTIVES

CHAPTER FIFTEEN

Ushering in a New Era

Megan Gardner, Founder of Independent & Co

Megan is a sought-after CEO advisor and board member for fast-growing technology businesses. A seasoned dealmaker, she is dedicated to helping CEOs navigate the challenges of rapid growth and celebrate entrepreneurial victories.

She founded Independent & Co in 2013, and the company's portfolio now spans North America, Europe, Asia, and Australia. Her focus is on high-growth technology companies, especially in the e-commerce, fintech, API/SaaS tools, and healthcare sectors. In just five years, her portfolio companies have successfully completed numerous rounds of fund-raising and several transactions, including a sale to Oracle and a public listing on the ASX.

As a business innovator, Megan focuses on applying disruptive technology to new spaces and teams. As CEO and founder of Plum District, Megan raised millions in venture capital, expanded the digital marketing company to two dozen cities, and grew the online member base to more than 1 million people. Megan managed more than 350 employees and contractors; worked with top retailers such as Target, Gap, and Whole Foods; and created partnerships with Facebook, Google, and Disney. Under her leadership, the company was featured in The New York Times, Wall Street Journal, *and* Bloomberg. Forbes *also repeatedly listed Plum District as one of ForbesWoman Top 100 Websites for Women.*

In 2011, Megan was nominated by Fortune as one of the Most Powerful Women Entrepreneurs. She regularly speaks at conferences, including the Wall Street Journal's Women in the Economy and TechWomen. Megan serves on a number of boards, including Tinybeans (ASX: TNY) and Crown & Caliber (chair). She operates as an independent board member and advisor for Apiary, Everly-Well, and others.

WHEN I JOINED YPO AT THE AGE OF THIRTY-SIX, I WAS the second youngest member to join my chapter. I had been thinking about YPO since my college days, when, as part of the Entrepreneurship Club at Harvard Business School, I had the opportunity to attend a dinner with some YPO members. I didn't realize at the time what a big deal this was—YPO hosts it every year at Harvard, and the seats are awarded by lottery. As a twenty-nine-year-old scholarship student for whom simply attending Harvard was a dream come true, I was excited just to be going to dinner with a group of CEOs. My interest was piqued.

Most impressive was the fact that the YPO guests were also excited to be there talking to us. A lot of people in YPO are CEOs, but many are in a family business or entrepreneurs who bootstrapped everything, so it was special for them to be at Harvard, too. The members we met were keenly interested in hearing our ideas and plans for businesses.

Now that I've become a mentor to students at Harvard, I understand why. It's very rewarding to talk to optimistic young people who are generating new ideas and could use advice from someone with more experience. These young people are ready to change the world. That's probably what the YPO folks saw in us that night, too.

Riding the Waves with YPO

Years later, after I had started a business called Plum District, some folks from YPO asked if I would be interested in joining the organization. It was humbling and an honor because I didn't feel I was anywhere near their level. My company was still very young at that time—maybe two years old. So was my marriage.

I was concerned because I had heard that the chapter closest to my home, the Golden Gate chapter, had only 10 percent women. I wouldn't have let that stop me, however. My biggest reservation was the time commitment. One of my board members even counseled against joining YPO, because she thought it would take too much time. I am so glad I didn't take that piece of advice.

The process of joining YPO isn't quick or easy. Members visited me, I attended lunches, and I had to fill out so much paperwork! I thought it was crazy at the time, but now I understand why YPO does all of this. YPO is a serious commitment, the group leaders want to ensure people are a good fit. YPO wants people who will be dedicated, because their peers already are.

At the time, I was busy scaling my business, a Groupon-type company focusing on families and moms. We had about 300 employees by then and a big infusion of capital. We were in twenty-plus cities, and our sales team was composed of stay-at-home moms working as part-time salespeople. We were trying to figure out how to grow and scale the organization.

As a new, young CEO who needed advice, it was the perfect time for me to join YPO. I remember coming into my first meeting with people who were much older than I was and running different and sometimes bigger businesses. I was in awe of the wealth of information in the room. I learned things I hadn't been taught in business school, such as when to break the "rules," move fast, and see what works. I didn't have that kind of perspective at the time, and I needed it badly, because our industry was growing rapidly.

I was struck by how much everyone in YPO had going on, regardless of how big their business was, how rich they were, or how put-together their lives seemed. I quickly discovered that it's not unusual for first-time CEOs to feel overwhelmed.

What *was* unique was my age. People loved to point out how much younger I was than most other members; some didn't take me seriously, but others did. I didn't spend too much time thinking about it. In some ways, the age range is something I love about YPO. In the United States, few of us live in close contact with other generations; we're often surrounded by people our own age in our neighborhoods or apartment buildings. Communicating closely with people who are in different places in life, both personally and professionally, has broadened my perspective.

In the years I've been a part of YPO, I've bought and sold five different companies, and I now work full time advising companies and serving on private and public boards. I turn to my chapter members when I need advice on deal structures and making hard management changes. Some of my closest friends are folks I met at YPO who are decades older than I am.

At the same time, the younger members of YPO keep things fresh. My current forum is constantly in communication. "Does anyone have a recruiter in this area?" "I'm looking at this particular company—has anyone met this guy?" The communication is constant.

Support in All Facets of Life

Spending all this time together in forums also helps members bond, which is invaluable when things threaten to rock your world. It's a grounding force to know you can go to your YPO "secret team." You can have conversations with them that you can't have with just anyone.

They were a true lifesaver when I developed a heart condition called peripartum cardiomyopathy when I was pregnant with my daughter. I found out about my condition about two weeks before my daughter was born. I was in the doctor's office, huffing and puffing, but I figured that was normal when nearly nine months pregnant. Plus, I was running a company, talking about selling, and worrying about the fund-raising environment. I assumed I was just stressed.

The doctor saw things differently. She made me go to the emergency room and then home for bed rest. I was terrified that I was going to die. I didn't go back to work, but because I had everything ready for my maternity leave already, my CFO was able to step in.

It was tough even after my daughter was born. I was a new mother with a rare heart condition, and I could barely lift my baby. The doctors wanted me to stop breastfeeding so that I could go on heart medication. There was little research on those medications because my condition is so rare. I didn't know what to do. In the midst of all of this, one of my chapter mates connected me with another chapter member, who got me in right away to see a top cardiologist at Stanford Hospital. I still thank that chapter member every time I see him.

Meanwhile, I had many business decisions to make: Do I keep running a company? Do I move on? One of my YPO forum mates gave me the best advice. She said to "try things on for a day." Her advice was that I not make huge decisions about everything all at once but try out different choices and see what each option looks and feels like. Try it on. See how it feels for a day. That was phenomenal advice and is something I pass on to others all the time.

I wanted to sell the business, but the board didn't. It took me about six months to sort out my health situation and multiple doctor appointments before things started to become more manageable. I decided not to return to the business. The CFO didn't want to stay, so the board brought in someone else and sold the company a few years later. I believe everything worked out exactly the way it was supposed to. My lesson from all of this is that you shouldn't wait to be diagnosed with a heart condition before you start taking better care of yourself.

YPO for the Family

My husband, Mike, joined the partner forum right after I joined YPO. Mike and I met in business school, and he also has a busy career—he was general manager of a large olive oil company and is now CEO of a chocolate company. YPO helped him in navigating his own career changes and business decisions. He could have spoken with friends or coworkers but not with the depth he was able to achieve with his forum.

For my husband and me, YPO has been a two-for-one experience. Mike has gotten as much out of it as I have. Without the partner forum, the dynamic in our marriage would have been strange, because the YPO forum is the core and cornerstone of YPO, and it's entirely confidential. You can't tell anyone else what happened during your forum meetings. It felt odd going to a four-hour meeting and not being able to talk about it with Mike, so it helps that he has his own forum to attend. We look forward to each other's forum dates, because we know we'll both have an opportunity to work through "stuff" with a peer group.

YPO is meant to be for the entire family, even the kids. YLAB is a great opportunity for older kids to peek behind the curtain and hear senior executives speak. They get to use and play with products and gain valuable exposure to business leadership. There are other family trips as well.

Your YPO experience is better when the whole family participates. I have even more fun at YPO events when my husband is there with me. We might have a nice dinner out or go to an event and then have an interesting conversation we can dig into together. We recently attended a parenting event, and my husband and I are still talking about the speaker and some of the things she said.

Serving as Chair

As I grew in YPO, I was frequently asked to serve as chair, but

I said no many times. Sitting on a nonprofit board threatened to eat up what remained of my increasingly precious time. My husband travels 150,000-plus miles per year, we have a small child, and we both have demanding careers. There isn't a lot of time left over.

And yet, people kept asking. Eventually, after my husband told me he supported the idea, I decided to go for it. I'm glad I did. It gave me a wonderful opportunity to practice using my skills as an influencer, because I had to work with more than seventy opinionated CEOs! It also gave me a chance to take our already-strong chapter to the next level.

Ultimately, I became chair because I realized you get out of YPO what you put into it. The more involved you are, the more you know people and the more you'll get out of it.

Changes

Those who spoke at that first dinner I attended at Harvard were mostly men. I remember talking with one woman from Greece—one of the only other women at the dinner. It's hard to believe, but when I started in YPO Golden Gate, there were still forums that wouldn't take women. In fact, even when I was forum chair, there were a number of forums that emphatically refused to take women. Things have changed, though. Since I've joined, we've grown from only 10 percent women in our chapter to 37 percent. The Golden Gate chapter has one of the highest percentages of women among YPO chapters around the world, and we were the first chapter globally to have all mixed-gender forums.

John Welch, the current chair of our chapter and a very funny guy, said in a recent meeting, "Let's just get this to fifty-fifty so we can stop talking about it." Amen to that!

We were able to implement mixed forums so quickly because there was interest from both the men and the women on the executive team. Also, the newest members had no interest in single-sex forums. That gave us additional momentum, because we could honestly tell the leaders of the single-sex forums that no one wanted to join them. There was a lot of energy around the goal; the only question was how long it would take. There are many women and people of color leading companies. We just had to seek them out.

The men were supportive of the effort, but the true leaders making this difference were mostly women. As things have evolved, even those opposed to the mixed-gender forums have changed their opinions as they've seen the benefits of diversity in the forums.

There is momentum around the push to include more diversity—women, millennials, people of color, politics, experiences, and the list goes on. In fact, the head of the international board of YPO invited me to breakfast recently to discuss the topic, and I recently participated in a session crafting YPO's diversity and inclusion strategy with a task force of diverse YPO members from around the world in conjunction with members of the YPO team, including the CEO. When people hear about what we're doing at Golden Gate, they want to know more about it.

CHAPTER SIXTEEN

The Value of Diversity

Kausik Rajgopal, Managing Partner at McKinsey & Company

Kausik is the managing partner of McKinsey's West Coast office and co-leads the firm's global fintech efforts.

Since joining McKinsey, Kausik has worked primarily in the financial services, payments, and fintech industries, helping banks, merchants, payments processors, and software and technology providers address strategy, operations, and organizational issues. He also leads the public sector practice on the West Coast with a focus on improving operations and successfully managing trans-formational change.

Outside of McKinsey, Kausik serves on the boards of the Bay Area Council, the San Francisco Symphony, the Commonwealth Club of California, and Stanford University's Graduate School of Business.

WHEN I JOINED YPO, I WAS EIGHT MONTHS INTO MY NEW role as a managing partner leading McKinsey's western region in the United States. I hoped that YPO forums would give me perspective on better integrating my professional and personal life. My kids were five and eight then, and I needed to find time for them and for my own health and wellness.

I came home from my first forum and told my wife that the group was exactly what I'd been looking for. While I could get perspectives from people in either my personal sphere or my professional life, YPO allowed me to get both perspectives in one place from a group of peers.

One of the first things my forum mates helped me with was a situation in which I had to have a tough performance feedback discussion. I'm a nice person who avoids conflict, so this was difficult for me. YPO helped me understand how to do that thoughtfully, cleanly, humanely, and in a relationship-oriented way.

I also quickly realized I couldn't BS in the forum. YPO peers have a high level of experience and pattern recognition, so you must pay attention and never tune out. There is nowhere to hide. We spend 95 percent of our lives in environments where we can hide parts of ourselves—where we avoid saying how we really feel—but this is not one of those places. These folks can spot BS from a mile away, and they won't tolerate it.

Four things make YPO forums a place where you can be yourself:

- **SELECTIVITY:** YPO's high bar for admission ensures you are in the company of peers. You respect every individual in the room and trust what they say.
- **EXPERIENCE:** Whether you're in a room with an entire chapter or just your forum, your fellow members' experience brings a richness that supports and empowers candor.

- **DIVERSITY:** The ideas you hear don't come from a single viewpoint. Gender diversity is particularly important to me.
- **CONFIDENTIALITY:** This is highly respected at YPO. Before I joined, I was given a lot of advice and perspective on what was important and what was unacceptable. There are consequences and sanctions, including expulsion from the forum and chapter, for violating confidentiality.

My wife's initial impression of YPO was that it was a good old boys' club, but that's not the case in our chapter. When I joined, our chapter chair, membership chair, and forum chair were all women, and chapter composition has grown to more than 37 percent women. This reassured my wife.

Leading Diversity

The Golden Gate chapter once had a low percentage of women in its membership but has since led the charge to improve gender diversity.

Our chapter is a global front-runner in this endeavor for a number of reasons. Our chapter members' networks are more gender diverse than those of other executives. Networks can be homogeneous or heterogeneous, and both types tend to perpetuate. This chapter has attracted members with diverse networks. Today, it is our chapter's norm to be diverse. A non-diverse room is an aberration.

When I joined, my forum was new, and we had only five members, all of whom were male. This was an exception to the norm for our chapter, so our forum asked the chapter to help us add female members. My forum has since added women, and it feels more natural now. There is something powerful about making diversity the default.

A Background in Diversity

Diversity is important to me. I grew up in India and came to the United States for college. I was often the only nonwhite person in the room, and I became sensitized to that dynamic. It isn't that I have horror stories of being rejected, but it is viscerally discomforting when you sit in a room and realize you are different from everyone else. As I became more senior, I began noticing that in many meetings, there was only one woman in a room of men, and I felt empathy toward that person. I knew she must likely feel the way I felt.

Part of my sensitivity to the issue stems from my own mother. I am the only child of a woman who had a college degree but did not work because her culture expected her to stay home and take care of me. My mother is one of the most empathetic, smart, organized, and amazing people I know, and I often reflect on the astounding loss of human capital that the world suffered because she never entered the workforce. So diversity, particularly from a gender standpoint, feels personal to me.

We all do better work in more diverse teams. A tech company CEO recently noted to me that it's become difficult to get visas for talented people to come to the United States. That company has since created a policy: if you're really smart, particularly if you're technically talented and can code well, the company will hire you anywhere. If you're in Nigeria, they'll take you on as a remote employee. The CEO believes teams that are diverse—not just in terms of gender but also national origin and sexual orientation—build better products.

This has been my experience as well. I try to work in gender-balanced teams. In the US western region, my company, McKinsey, has more than doubled its percentage of women in our incoming class from 24 percent in 2012 to 50 percent this year. We also worked with the Clayman Institute for Gender Research at Stanford to better understand and begin addressing our unconscious biases. That has made a big difference.

Balancing Life

In the past year, YPO has helped me balance my life. YPO gave me perspective on prioritizing the big rocks over the little pebbles in my life. I spend less time worrying about little things.

Having the perspective of my forum and chapter members has made me more accountable to this commitment to operate differently. For example, I made a commitment that whenever I was in town, I would spend unstructured free time with my family in the afternoons. Before, I was squeezing my family into the margins of my professional calendar. YPO also helped me destress and uncomplicate the choices I was wrestling with—such as whether we should send our son to public or private school.

My forum mates at YPO have helped me shift my mindset. I grew up in a family with high standards and expectations. I was often at the top of my class. I have always correlated high standards with hard work, but YPO helped me learn how to have high standards without feeling like I have to be at 100 percent all of the time.

One of my most significant takeaways from YPO is best summed up by a quote from Maya Angelou: "I've learned that people will forget what you said, people will forget what you did, but people will never forget how you made them feel." In dealing with situations in my life, whether it's a tough professional conversation or a debate with my spouse over one of our kids, I remember that the other person will not remember what I said or how I said it, but they will remember how I made them feel.

The True Benefits of Membership

The time commitment to YPO initially seemed like extra pressure, but I learned that the juice is worth the squeeze. If I were to advise anyone, particularly a CEO who is having that same reservation about the time commitment, I would tell them to spend time with people in YPO to understand what we get out of the organization. When you do that, it's much easier to decide if it's worth it. Describing what it's like to be in the YPO forums is a little like describing chocolate; whatever you say will be only a tiny fraction as effective as tasting the chocolate itself.

I am now the moderator of my forum. This is a big responsibility and has opened my eyes to the greater benefits of membership. As a moderator, I'm also on the membership committee, and it's exciting to see the quality of the candidates who come and share their inspirational stories. It's an unexpected benefit. Being on the membership committee, taking moderator training, and connecting with other moderators outside my forum are all undervalued dimensions of YPO.

Sitting in membership committee meetings and trying to decide if a candidate would be a good fit is much different than sharing perspective in forums. You get to know people in a different way, and I have grown to appreciate these additional experiences.

In addition to my forum experience, the chapter has been rewarding, too. We had a Chinese New Year event that was beautifully done. We also visited San Quentin prison with members of YPO Gold, and everyone was crying by the end. The chapter events are designed with a lot of care and attention, with real ownership, and they make you feel like you're a part of something truly special.

CHAPTER SEVENTEEN

Devoted to Diversity

Mac Harman, Founder of Balsam Hill

In 2006, Mac founded the Balsam Hill brand in his Palo Alto, California, apartment and coordinated a group of partners that revolutionized the Christmas tree industry. Today, he works with colleagues and partners around the world to lead the strategic direction of his company and its products. He retains his role as the lead designer of each of Balsam Hill's Christmas trees and travels the world in search of the finest products to share with Balsam Hill's customers.

I'M PASSIONATE ABOUT THE TOPIC OF DIVERSITY, SO when I looked into YPO, I was keenly interested in whether it valued diversity. I was not looking for some cigar-smoking, scotch-drinking boys' club.

I was very clear at all steps of the YPO application process that I was interested not only in a diverse forum but also in a diverse forum agenda as well. I specifically asked for a co-ed forum. At the time I joined, I was placed in a forum with three women, which was the most in our chapter and was probably abnormally large compared to other chapters.

Why do I consider diversity such a seminal issue? I'm a white male, and while discrimination doesn't necessarily involve me, I've seen what bias looks like. My wife is Korean American, and we have three mixed-ethnicity children. I've been in all-white settings where people make derogatory comments about Asian people, not knowing that my wife is Asian American, and I've seen people staring at my wife and me holding hands in public. I didn't invite my own grandparents to my wedding because they didn't support my marriage. My mother-in-law, meanwhile, grew up with a boy's name that her progressive dad gave her so she wouldn't face discrimination on paper.

After my father died and I began overseeing his manufacturing company, the day-to-day manager of the plant was once turned away from a restaurant because one of the employees he was taking out to lunch was black. To me, this was a wake-up call. This incident happened in 2004 and occurred in a restaurant across the street from the hospital where I was born. More recently, I excused myself from a hot tub at a hotel in British Columbia after hearing the two other occupants—both white males—discuss how Asian people had ruined Vancouver.

These instances anger me, but more importantly, they disappoint me. I don't want to be in a place or belong to a group that discriminates. This is one reason why YPO was attractive to me: I could see the members shared my sensibilities and were willing to work hard to correct some of these injustices through encouraging and learning from diversity.

However, I still feel we have a lot of work to do.

Growing Up in Cleveland

To understand my focus on diversity, it helps to know my background. I grew up in suburban Cleveland, and though the city is known for having racial tension, ours was an all-white neighborhood. I didn't meet a single person of Asian descent until high school.

I grew up comfortably in a nice part of the blue-collar, hardscrabble side of town. We were better off than many of my friends' families but not as well off as others in my parents' circle of friends. My dad ran a little factory that wasn't particularly profitable. If he had an especially good year, we would go on a special beach vacation; if he didn't, we wouldn't. I also saw the impact economic realities had on my friends. If someone's parent got laid off from the Ford Motor plant graveyard shift, it was a great hardship for them. In many ways, my upbringing gave me the ability to put myself in other people's shoes and not to take resources and opportunities for granted.

I was very entrepreneurial as a child. When I was three, I went door to door in our neighborhood with my Radio Flyer wagon, selling old tennis balls as dog toys. One year, I grew gourds from a packet of seeds I received as a favor at a birthday party and put up a gourd retail stand in my front yard. Unfortunately, they did not sell well. That's when I realized that when you're on a dead-end street, populated by people over seventy who only leave their houses once a week to get groceries, selling inedible gourds is not a good business plan. Later, I set up a lemonade stand on the busier cross street to my sleepy street, but when I noticed that cars had trouble finding space to pull over to buy something, I loaded my products up in the good ol' Radio Flyer and, once again, went door to door. That was much more successful. It turns out that people in their seventies have a hard time saying no to a cute seven-year-old selling lemonade on their doorstep.

Eventually, I moved on to washing cars and mowing lawns, but then, I started high school at an academically challenging Jesuit school, and I no longer had time for entrepreneurial pursuits. In fact, I got so involved in organizations throughout high school and my years at Williams College that I forgot I was entrepreneurial. I didn't even remember it when I entered Stanford Business School after college.

Going away to Williams and Stanford was eye-opening because I was surrounded by such a mix of people: classmates who were there on full-ride financial aid contrasted with classmates who were wealthier than anyone I knew growing up. College was also much more ethnically diverse than my high school.

Starting a Business

After my first year at Stanford, I decided to start my own business while working at an eleven-week internship at Clorox. I loved Clorox, but the internship helped me realize that I didn't want to work for a big company. I knew that ninety-nine out of one hundred entrepreneurial ventures fail—those CEOs coming to speak to us at Stanford were the 1 percent who made it—but it felt like the right time to start. I was married, but we didn't have kids or a mortgage, and my wife was working one-hundred-plus hours per week training as a physician. I wouldn't be seeing her much anyway, so why not throw myself into this new business idea? I graduated from Stanford and gave myself six months to come up with a business idea. If it didn't work out, I'd go back to one of my previous employers or find something else to do.

I developed an idea that I thought might work. However, I didn't want to take venture capital for my startup—I wanted to be in full control of the business. So I decided to start a side project to fund my main idea. My side project was selling artificial Christmas trees on the internet.

BalsamHill.com opened for business on October 1, 2006, and by the end of the first year, we'd made almost $3 million in revenue. It took off so quickly that I had to put my main idea on pause to manage the side project!

I was focused on hiring a great team that could take over when I went back to my main business idea. One of my first hires was Caroline, an Asian American Stanford classmate I knew well. It took a long time to persuade her to come on board, but I told her that when she was ready, she could take over as CEO.

"I will help out," I said. "I won't leave you hanging, but when you take over, I'll go back to my other business."

That was my plan. As with most entrepreneurial ventures, however, things never really follow the plan. Today, Caroline serves as our COO, and we are both part of a talented group of women and men who have led us to over $150 million in revenue in North America, Europe, and Australia.

The Challenges of Being a CEO

I know firsthand how difficult it is to be a CEO. The CEO must always set the tone. You may be tired because your infant kept you up all night, but everyone is still expecting you to have a good attitude and the right answer. When you're a CEO, slip-ups can have a huge negative impact.

When things go wrong, no matter how it happened, it's always ultimately the CEO's fault. That is the constant pressure that comes with being the leader. You don't get normal breaks or a complete mental vacation like most people. I am quite good at segregating my time and compartmentalizing things, but I rarely take a vacation where I don't check my phone at least once per day. You're always on call.

For example, in 2017, Balsam Hill partnered with a vendor to open several pop-up retail stores in New Jersey. Months after the stores closed, the state of New Jersey sued me personally, claiming that I violated their statute regarding refund policies. I had no idea what the lawsuit was about. It turns out that New Jersey requires brick-and-mortar retail stores to post their refund policy in each store, and one of our stores did not do so. The citation originally had been sent to the wrong address, and we never received it—so instead of paying a simple $500 fine, I was ordered to appear in court in New Jersey. At the time, my wife and I were about to refinance our home, and this lawsuit could have prevented the loan's approval. The lawsuit was eventually dismissed, but the minor anxiety it caused is typical of one of the many concurrent stresses CEOs bear each day.

Women CEOs

As difficult as it is to be CEO, I think about how much more difficult it is for women CEOs.

For instance, although I am deeply involved in raising our three kids, I've never had to find a place in the office to pump breastmilk, like some female CEOs might. If I go speak somewhere, I'll bring slacks and a shirt, or maybe a tie and a sports coat, depending on where I'm speaking. I don't have to bring makeup or get up fifteen minutes earlier to apply it. I'm not expected to cover up wrinkles or do my hair perfectly; I don't reserve time to get my nails done or eyebrows waxed.

No one judges me for not doing those things. But if a female CEO chooses not to wear makeup or wears the same dress two days in a row, that may not work out as well for her. When I give a speech on stage, I'm not doing it in three-inch heels. I don't have to worry about my stiletto getting stuck in a crack in the stage, although I saw that happen to a female friend.

I have dedicated a lot of thought to the challenges women face in the workplace. I make sure our offices have a lactation suite with sound insulation and a private fridge to help women feel more comfortable and to make the interruptions from pumping less inconvenient. Anytime we look at new offices for our company, I walk to the nearest public transportation stop to make sure an employee would feel safe walking to or from this stop in the dark.

I try to make sure we are not passively discriminating or engaging in accidental bias. When I learned through a YPO forum mate how specific job descriptions appeal more to male applicants, I took the information back to my team. We rewrote our job descriptions to use less male-oriented wording and expanded the required language about nondiscrimination to include more welcoming language, such as "we are dedicated to diversity."

Thinking about gender diversity is a start, but we need to walk the talk. I'm proud that Balsam Brands' leadership team has always included more women than men. At one point, we actively recruited mothers of twins who were returning to work after taking extended time off. Other companies wouldn't "take the risk" on them, because they'd been out of the workforce longer than other parents, but their competence, efficiency, and patience made these mothers extremely valuable to our company.

Similarly, we believe that an ethnically diverse workforce makes us stronger as a company, and we have recruited a diverse workforce to our domestic locations. This includes many immigrants because we sponsor many visas as a small company. I am disappointed that we don't currently have any African American employees, although we do have employees from multiple African countries, including one who came here as a refugee.

Our biggest challenge is encouraging diversity in our Boise, Idaho, office. Boise is not yet a very diverse city, but the mayor and the economic development agency have actively worked with me to attract a more ethnically diverse population. To its credit, Boise is one of the leading cities in the United States in welcoming refugees, and that effort goes back to the seventies. We are all working together to build on this for the future.

Focus on the Customer

Diversity makes sense from a business standpoint, too. How can you understand your customers' needs if no one on your team can relate to them?

Once, when I was at a consulting firm early in my career, I found myself sitting in a conference room, drawing a picture of a tampon and talking about the components of it with two other guys. No one had a clue what is in a tampon or how it works. I thought, "Our client is paying us a lot of money to figure out what a tampon is, and we are wasting their time."

I left the room and walked over to the division CEO's executive assistant, who was in her late sixties, and explained our dilemma. "I know this is going to sound weird, but we are in this room trying to figure out tampons—how they're made and how they work—and I think we're wasting your company's money guessing," I said. "Can you please help us?"

That was a risky thing for me to do at the age of twenty-three, but this woman cracked a wry smile and helped. She drew a picture and explained it to me, and I took the picture back into the room. I also left with a good lesson: if you want to do things right, make sure you have a good mix of perspectives in the room.

Spreading Joy, Not Religion

Diversity also applies to religious beliefs. I sell Christmas trees and happen to be an actively practicing Christian, but I don't think Christmas trees are exclusively a Christian symbol. Jesus didn't have a Christmas tree, and according to some sources, the origins of the symbol are pagan. Our company is focused on spreading joy, and we welcome all who share our values, including people of different faiths.

Early on in the business, I tried to launch a pop-up store in one of the top-grossing malls in the country (in dollars per square foot). This mall in Palo Alto, California, rarely has vacancies, and I didn't even have a product to show, just a sample branch.

The mall manager said I could talk to the person who did the temporary leasing, and I drove through three hours of traffic and road construction to persuade her to take us. I walked into her office, and the first words out of the woman's mouth were, "I'm Jewish." Immediately I thought, *Great, I just wasted a day coming to see her.* She then continued, "And I love Christmas trees." That was how I learned about how many Jews love Christmas trees. Today, we sell Christmas trees to people of all faiths. Christmas trees are popular in Dubai, for example. It would be silly for our company to disregard any religious persuasion in our quest to share joy and bring friends and family together in celebration.

We had one person withdraw her application from us because she thought we were a "Christian company." I'm sure we have had other people do the same because we are a Christmas tree company. These folks might be surprised to learn that we used to have a Jewish person on our leadership team and that I have Jewish, Muslim, and Hindu colleagues. One Jewish colleague wrote a note to us that said, "I just wanted to let you know that I almost didn't apply here because I'm Jewish, but I decided to anyway. I am so glad I did. I feel so welcome here."

That is a real testament to our company's culture.

Back to YPO

So you can see why I want YPO chapters to be diverse, even if they're in a predominately white city like Boise. I attended a national YPO event recently and met a woman from the East Coast who couldn't believe we had co-ed forums and chapters that are 37 percent women. She said there were very few women in her chapter. What a loss for the men not to have insights from women, and what a challenge that must be for the few women who are likely called upon in their forums to represent the views of all women.

We've learned in our chapter that women are the best at recruiting other women, and it is difficult to persuade women to join when they don't see others who are already making the commitment. I'm hopeful that East Coast woman's chapter can make bold strides to increase its gender diversity. I also hope that YPO as a whole will move in the same direction as the Golden Gate chapter. It's clear from a recent "Women in YPO" event that I attended that YPO is committed to this globally. Once we get all the other hundreds of chapters closer to where our chapter and some others are, YPO and its members will benefit greatly.

I'll soon be moving into the position of membership chair in our chapter, and I have already planted seeds with other members for bringing in more diversity. We have specific goals for membership. You can't go after everything at once, of course, but we are making progress. Even though ethnic diversity isn't a specific goal, four of the last seven people we admitted were not white. One of our goals next year may end up being to increase ethnic diversity or specifically recruit underrepresented minorities, and we've made a good start.

Even as it strives to change, YPO remains an incredible support group. YPO allows leaders who have a lot on their shoulders to talk not just about work but also about personal issues and family. The more diversity we have in our forums and in our chapters, the more we can all learn and grow.

CHAPTER EIGHTEEN

Trailblazing in Male Environments

Christa Quarles, CEO of OpenTable

Christa was the chief executive officer of OpenTable, Inc., from August 2015 to December 2018. She previously held the role of chief financial officer. Before joining OpenTable, Christa was the chief business officer for Nextdoor and held positions of increasing responsibility with the Walt Disney Company, ranging from senior vice president to head of business operations. Before that, she was a successful Wall Street analyst covering internet and technology companies.

THE MAJORITY OF MY EARLY CAREER WAS SPENT WORKING on Wall Street. Originally an internet research analyst, I decided to stop armchair quarterbacking and instead find a company where I could help build something. I struggled to find the right role and, frankly, to find someone who would take a risk on someone like me who had never held an operating role. John Pleasants, who ran Ticketmaster and parts of Electronic Arts, was that someone. After becoming my boss, he introduced me to YPO. I saw that John—a leader, boss, and someone I respected—benefited from his membership, but I wasn't eligible to join at that point.

By the fall of 2015, I had become CEO of OpenTable, and the idea of joining YPO started to pop up again. Many chapters wanted more diversity, so the ones in the Bay Area started reaching out to me. I had to figure out the differences between the different chapters and pick the one that best suited me. It was a little overwhelming. I then met Cara France at a Marketers That Matter event OpenTable hosted. We joke even to this day that she was relentless in encouraging me to consider her YPO chapter from the moment she realized I qualified. As soon as she said, "We have the best women," I was sold. That was vital for me, because the last thing I wanted to be was woman number two or a super-minority in a group of mostly male professionals. I had no desire to be the maverick in a forum. If I was going to join, I wanted a group that had already set that precedent. I was tired of being the token woman at the table. I had no interest in being the trailblazer for this chapter in my life.

I had already been trailblazing for my entire career.

Finding Psychological Safety

My first job out of college was on Wall Street working at the Merrill Lynch bond desk. Many of the characters from *Liar's Poker* were scattered across the trading floor. They had outlawed strippers on the trading floor a couple of years before, but it was still a very male, aggressive environment. I went to Harvard Business School, which was 70 percent male, and then worked at Thomas Weisel Partners, where I was the second female partner out of sixty-five partners. Finally, I worked in the gaming industry, which is as male as anything I have ever seen. It wasn't until I worked for the Walt Disney Company in 2010 that I was in a room that was at least half women. It was the first time in my life I experienced a gender-balanced workforce.

In the early phases of my career, I acted like a man to be accepted by men. I didn't bring my whole self to work because I thought to get ahead, I needed to be domineering, aggressive, and never vulnerable. I'm fortunate now to be in a mixed-gender forum that has four women and five men. I no longer have to show up as a man.

But old habits die hard. One day, none of the other women were able to attend my YPO forum, so it was just me and five guys. I had just come from a Board Room in Crisis event hosted by Deloitte and JP Morgan, during which we discussed the frustrating phenomenon in mixed-gender boardrooms when a woman will make a comment that is ignored and then two minutes later, a man says the same thing and everyone listens. Experiences like these are insidious, because our ability to lead is undermined when we feel we can't bring our whole selves into a situation. If we aren't authentic, we can't represent ourselves in the way we need to as leaders.

The men in my forum are amazing, forward-thinking, and empathetic Renaissance men, but going into the forum that day as the only woman triggered many of my past unpleasant experiences, and I resorted to old habits. I felt myself puffing out my chest and doing all the weird peacockery that I used to do. I put on the persona of "I'm not going to show any vulnerability and am going to prove how tough I am."

Google once did a study on high-functioning teams and found that the number one criterion is psychological safety. If you don't feel safe, your prefrontal cortex shuts down, and your lizard brain takes over, which doesn't allow you to function optimally. I became aware that this was what was happening to me. I realized that if I didn't show any vulnerability, then I wasn't going to get much out of the experience. Eventually, I settled down. Because I meditate a lot, I'm in the habit of noticing when I'm feeling off. In this case, I was able to observe and acknowledge what I was doing and then move on.

Diversity Benefits Everyone

I spoke at *Fortune* this summer, catching the company up on what had happened in the year since the #MeToo movement went mainstream. The previous year, I stood up at the same conference and called bullshit on the notion that women in Silicon Valley weren't supportive of one another. As a result, I have become a bit of an accidental feminist on this topic.

After the event, a man who is a venture capitalist told me about an experience he had as the only man on a five-person board. He said, "I think every man in Silicon Valley should have to experience this because, for as much as I had thought I understood diversity, I had never really experienced what it felt like to be a minority." He mentioned how alone he felt, because he felt like he couldn't add anything to the conversations these women were having. He added that they were wonderful and kind women, and he knew they didn't intend to exclude him on purpose, but that he still felt left out. He said, "It hit me in a deeply visceral way—all the things that women have been saying, I finally felt." The sad fact is that every single woman I know has felt this feeling. And minority women doubly so.

It's not that men in general don't care; in my experience, it's that they haven't *felt* it. They can't relate. I worked with a male speech coach on my presentation for *Fortune*, and even he admitted that he didn't understand our challenges until he worked with me. "I consider myself a pretty progressive guy," he said, "but in working with you on this speech, I've learned about biases I didn't even know I had. This whole experience has been so eye-opening."

It's a Leadership Issue

YPO is the backbone of how business gets done and how relationships are formed. If women can overcome the barriers to entry, we'll be at the epicenter of power structures that have existed for a very long time. While I wasn't interested in being a trailblazer, anytime you get into a position of power, responsibility comes with it. This isn't a woman's issue or a man's issue; it's a leadership issue. Once you find yourself in a position of leadership, you have the power and the responsibility to change the rules of the game because now you're the one in charge.

My husband was in the military, and when all the sexual harassment claims started, he was very matter-of-fact about it. He said, "In the navy, when the commanding officers let it happen, it happened. The ones who didn't let it happen—that's where it didn't happen. It's that straightforward." Both the leaders who let it happen and the leaders who didn't set the tone for their unit; it's pretty cut and dried.

If a leader doesn't care about an issue, nothing is going to happen. They will come up with 1,500 excuses about why that is, but do they have those same 1,500 excuses when they don't meet their numbers? They will always come up with a way to meet their numbers, no matter what is standing in their way. Not only that, but it's well known that creating a more diverse and inclusive workforce will help you meet those numbers; one could argue it's a precondition for success.

YPO Sets the Stage

Diversity is critical everywhere but especially so in an organization like YPO. This is where the leaders meet; it's where power brokers live. If you can infiltrate this group with the idea that diversity is beneficial—if you can demonstrate from the inside out how well an inclusive environment works and how successful it is—it sets the stage for progress in the greater world.

One of the vital components of this evolution is men. We can't make changes unless men are a meaningful part of the journey. We live in a crazy, mixed-up world where men are often afraid to speak. We must make space for them and acknowledge that they're a vital part of the path of progress. One piece of advice I would give to men is to sit down with a woman and ask to hear her story. Build and gain empathy so that you can be a better leader and drive more diverse and inclusive workforces.

We see change in the many voices of men who are actively pursuing more women in membership. These men see the value in diversity and want it. How do we get the rest to care? I often make the argument that diversity is not just good for women—it's good for the bottom line. Heterogeneous groups have the best outcomes: diversity is the best angle to get large groups to come on board.

There is also a generational component to this shift. I'm forty-five, and when I look at women who are sixty-five, I know that they have had it much harder. They had to deal with overt bias. That sixty-five-year-old woman always had to deal with being "the only" in a group. She had to deal with the scarcity of women in the workplace that caused women to compete with one another instead of helping one another. The question is, what is the next generation going to look like? How will we help pave the way?

Righting the Ecosystem

Gold medalist soccer player Abby Wambach said that when she was coming up the ranks as a woman, she was told to be like Little Red Riding Hood—to stay on the path and do the right thing. In her speech to a graduating class at Barnard College, Wambach said that women shouldn't be Little Red Riding Hood anymore; instead, they should be wolves. She then talked about the reintroduction of wolves into Yellowstone. At first, people were unsure and afraid. What happened, though, was when the wolves began to increase in number, the flora and fauna started to come into balance, and populations of big and small game were normalized. The addition of wolves corrected the entire ecosystem within the park.

When you think about our current political environment, also consider the fact that women make up only 20 percent of the donor pool to political causes. It's because they don't control the money. Our ecosystem is out of balance. Looking toward the next generation, I'm very excited, because their tolerance for things I readily accepted coming up the ranks is very low. McKinsey did a study that said if women were able to work the same types of jobs, earn the same wages, and work the same number of hours as men, the world would be $28 trillion richer. That number represents the combined GDP of Germany, Japan, and the United States. Men would be richer, too, if women were in equal positions.

Sometimes gender diversity is viewed as an "I win, you lose" situation, but it's not that at all. Everyone is better when women are on equal footing. We all win.

Embracing Vulnerability

Personally, my forum feels like nirvana to me. There is something exceptional about being able to bring my whole self to a mixed-gender forum. There is a richness to the group that I haven't experienced elsewhere. My forum is not afraid to be vulnerable with one another, and we share everything.

One of the biggest benefits of my forum is that I have a self-help-on-demand texting service. For example, after I announced my intention to leave OpenTable, my forum served as a near-24/7 support line. We talked about the best way to approach my situation. I was able to tap into an immediate source of reliable anecdotes and inspiration.

It's lonely at the top—yes, it's a cliché, but it's also very true. I have my friends, my sisters, and other people I can talk to, but we don't have the shared experience of being the person at the top. At YPO, on the other hand, I can approach my forum when I have to let someone go or make a difficult financial decision, and they always share lessons from their own experience. They might be from a different industry, but they still understand what it means to set the culture, vision, and values of an organization. They understand the implications of something going right or wrong, selling a business, and so on. I don't feel lonely anymore, because I have this group of people behind me.

Before YPO, if I'd had an issue, I would turn inward. I would hold on to the anxiety and the stress, and my health would suffer as a result. It is essential for CEOs and presidents to have a place to vent that anxiety and feel supported. Without that, it just lives in you. I would likely bring that stress and anxiety home with me, which would then impact my children and my husband. YPO offers a place to share and productively work through these emotions in a safe environment.

YPO Made Me a Better Leader

During my exit speech at OpenTable, I said, "The minute you embrace your vulnerability, you become the most powerful person in the room." All the experiences of vulnerability that YPO has facilitated for me have made me a better leader, one that people want to follow and interact with.

The decision to leave OpenTable was a big one, and my forum mates helped me process the decision fully. The structure of my corporate entity was changing in a meaningful way, and it meant that OpenTable wasn't really going to be OpenTable, as a wholly independent and defined entity, anymore. It was going to be merged with another brand sitting inside our holding company. Functionally speaking, it was a merger.

I was able to immediately draw upon those in my forum who had gone through a merger or a sale of their business. There were quite a lot of experiences to be shared. One of the early pieces of advice given to me was that there would be a grieving process and that I needed to allow myself to grieve. My vision and dream for what this business would become was different now, and I had to let that go. We always encourage one another to experience emotions, to grieve when we've lost a loved one, or a business, or anything that makes you sad. As a CEO, some-times you feel like you can't indulge in anything resembling a "woe is me" feeling, but it is healthy to express those emotions in a safe place. If you're feeling sadness, anger, or frustration and hear about others who have also experienced those things, it's easier to work through them.

I worked at OpenTable for almost four years. I have the type of personality that is always compelled to sprint toward the next thing. This time, my YPO forum stepped in and encouraged me to slow down and make sure I chose the "right thing" not just the "next thing." This was particularly hard for me because opportunities and ideas were coming in fast. My forum gave me perspective, though. They reminded me that making the wrong decision would have many more far-reaching consequences than waiting to make the right one.

Leaving a business is always bittersweet. Future opportuni-ties are exciting to think about, but leaving the people you've worked with can be hard. When I left OpenTable, the out-pouring of emotion toward me was overwhelming. I had people tell me I was the best CEO they'd ever had. I received letters from people within the organization I didn't personally know. It was a true privilege to know I have touched so many lives. Looking forward, it's important to me that I find an opportu-nity in which I can work toward something that has an even greater impact. Working as a leader doesn't just mean you shape the business; you're also shaping people's lives.

Right now, I am exploring and learning. I've been learning about new businesses and spending time with investors, recruiters, and venture capitalists. It has been fun to learn and discover different things. I recognize that I am privileged to have this opportunity. There are so many choices, and I want to make sure I'm in a position to have the greatest impact.

With the help of my experience at YPO, regardless of where I end up, I know I will be ready to take charge and lead the way.

A World of Impact

THERE IS NOT A LOT OF WARMTH IN THE TERM "PRO-fessional organization." And while YPO is that, it's also so much more.

It is the place where 26,000 of the brightest, most prolific, and most visionary leaders in the world today have the freedom, space, and safety to explore, learn, and grow. Most importantly, it is the place where they can speak freely and be vulnerable. It is where they can be equal parts leader and human being. There are not many places like that today in general—and the more prestigious your job and high-powered your position, the more difficult those environments are to find.

While this book includes eighteen personal stories about the ways YPO has impacted the professional and personal lives of leaders today, it is still only a small glimpse into the impact YPO has had around the globe. Each person who is a part of YPO—both today and throughout the nearly seventy years since its inception—has their own story to tell about how this organization matters.

ACKNOWLEDGMENTS

Thank you to my seventeen fellow YPO members showcased in this book, who offered their precious time and personal stories—"on the record"—in the hope of impacting YPO chapters and future members around the globe.

It is not by accident YPO Golden Gate continues to redefine what is possible. Jiggs Davis, the co-founder of the Golden Gate chapter, started forums more than forty years ago, forever changing the YPO experience around the world.

Valli Benesch courageously became the first female member of the Golden Gate chapter in 1985, joined over the next decade by Dianne Snedaker (1988), Anne Bakar (1991), Sarah Nolan (1991), and Robin Wolaner (1995). These pioneering women led extraordinary companies at a time when women leaders faced significant headwinds, in and out of YPO.

In 1997, Dianne Snedaker served as the first female chapter chair, and in 2004, Kim Polese served as its first female membership officer, planting seeds of change throughout the chapter. During this time, David Mahoney helped navigate the chapter through the dot-com bust of 2000, keeping it strong at a time when many Bay Area companies simply "disappeared" overnight.

A decade later, the efforts of Mari Baker (membership officer 2010; chapter chair 2014) and Elizabeth Hutt Pollard (membership officer 2011–2013) changed the face of the YPO Golden Gate chapter. Under their leadership, the chapter doubled from

10 percent female members in 2010 to 21 percent by 2014, contributing to Elizabeth being elected to the YPO Global Board of Directors and Mari being elected as the YPO Gold Pacific US Regional Chair.

Elizabeth and Mari's efforts to recruit great women built on the great work of chapter chairs Evan Marwell (2010), Mark Jung (2011), and Eric Lindberg (2012), who shepherded our chapter through "Ages to Stages," when Golden Gate said goodbye to one-third of the chapter as they graduated into a newly created YPO Gold chapter.

A few years later, the collaboration of the trifecta of Megan Gardner (chapter chair 2017), Leah Solivan (membership officer 2017, 2018), and myself (forum officer 2016, 2017) led to Golden Gate reaching 37 percent female members and becoming the first chapter in YPO history to have all mixed-gender forums, establishing a new status quo that we hope other chapters will emulate.

This book went from idea to reality with the support of Megan Gardner (chapter chair 2017) and John Welch (chapter chair 2018) along with our chapter admin, Masie Amon, whose grace and competence help us reach new heights.

Thank you to the countless volunteers who serve as day chairs, officers, and forum moderators, keeping our chapter strong.

And finally, thank you to my extraordinary husband, Scott France, who exemplifies a person of substance, unwavering in his support and love for twenty-five years. And to our beautiful children, Tandara and Gabriel, who give our lives purpose each and every day.

CARA FRANCE

23786157R00125